ACES HIGH

By

Louise E. Ducharme

ISBN: 0-7596-8605-X

This book is printed on acid free paper.

1stBooks - rev. 06/19/02

ACKNOWLEDGEMENTS

Special thanks to:

Phyllis Ducharme, my sister-in-law, for her valuable contributions to this book.

and

My husband, Richard, for his support in his own special way.

Chapter One

"How would you like to be first lady?" Brenner asked.

Jennie scowled. "What are you talking about?"

"I may run for president."

The cup of coffee she was holding crashed to the floor.

The housekeeper put the coffeepot down and dashed to her side. "I'll take care of it."

"Sorry, for being so clumsy, Martha," Jennie said. "It just slipped out of my hand."

"No problem, ma'am."

Martha scooped up the broken pieces with care and went into the kitchen to dispose of them.

Jennie turned and glared at her husband. "You weren't serious about wanting to be president, Brenner."

"I'm considering it. What do you think?"

The phone rang and interrupted her response. Brenner hurried past Jennie to answer it.

"Sands, here."

His hands trembled and his face paled. "I'll be right there."

Jennie stared at him. "What's wrong?"

With downcast eyes he said, "It's Mike Ryan. He's dead."

"How terrible! What happened?"

"I'm not sure."

Brenner made a few calls and grabbed his coat.

"I've got to go to the club and tell the others. I may be late so don't wait up for me."

"Please be careful driving."

He nodded and hurried out the door.

Brenner took a few deep breaths, climbed into his black Mercedes Benz, and drove down the highway to the outskirts of Washington, D.C. Fifteen minutes later he parked in back of a ten-story building that was set back off the road. A security officer stopped him outside to check his identification.

Once inside he displayed his government I.D. to another officer. "I've been coming here for ten years. Don't you guys know me by now?"

"Just routine, sir."

"Damn bureaucratic routines," grumbled Brenner.

He walked up to a door with a sign that said, 'Government Officials.' He thrust the door open, scanned the room, and sat down at a table with several other men.

All of them were members of congress and close friends. They were referred to as the Aces High poker players. For the past five years they met every Wednesday at the club and played cards while they drank, talked, and laughed together.

Raymond spoke first. "We never meet on Fridays. What's up?"

Peter's green eyes were solemn. "Should I tell them?"

"No, I will," said Brenner as he stood before the group.

"Hold on a minute," Johnny said. "Mike's missing. Aren't we going to wait for him?"

Brenner's broad shoulders drooped. "Mike won't be here."

"Why not?"

"Because he's…dead."

"No way," Johnny said.

Bruce was wide-eyed. "Can't believe it."

"It's true," Brenner said. "His wife found him dead in bed this morning."

"How did he die?" asked Chuck.

"Appears to be from natural causes," said Brenner. "Dr. Levin's doing an autopsy to find out what happened."

"He wasn't sick when we played poker with him Wednesday," Raymond said.

Chuck shook his head. "He didn't look good to me."

"I was worried about him," Peter said. "When I asked him how he felt, he told me he had a little cold."

Chuck brushed back his sandy hair that was highlighted with gray and frowned. "Doesn't sound serious enough to kill him."

"What a shock," Bruce said.

They appeared dumbfounded while they gazed into space.

Johnny stood up. "Who wants a drink?"

"I sure could use one," said Chuck.

In a few minutes Johnny returned with drinks for everyone. His short, stout body trembled and beads of perspiration were visible on his forehead when he passed them out.

Brenner raised his glass and said, "Here's to you, Mike, wherever you are. We're going to miss you."

Raymond's dark eyes became misty while he lifted his glass. "You were here with us every week. It won't be the same without you, guy."

One by one they toasted Mike and reminisced on their good times together.

They were sipping another drink when Chuck said, "That could happen to any of us." His eyes traveled around the table. "Think about it…we're all about the same age."

Peter shrugged and looked at his watch. "It's getting late…time to go."

"I'm on my way, too," said Johnny.

They all left in different directions.

Twenty minutes later, Brenner carefully climbed into his bed.

Jenny snuggled close to him. "How did it go?"

"Let's talk about it in the morning."

She put her arm around his waist and pressed her body against his.

Brenner pulled her hand away. "Bad timing."

"I was only trying to comfort you."

"Sure you were," he said as he moved closer to the wall.

Jennie had a strong urge to be held...loved by her husband. Feeling discouraged, she got up and tiptoed into the guestroom.

She pulled out a bureau drawer, groped under some clothes, and grasped a bottle of whiskey. After gulping down two full glasses of the liquor, her body started to relax.

Soft music played in the background while Jennie read a passionate romantic novel. A short time later, she drifted into a blissful sleep.

Chapter Two

With trembling hands, Bruce Rivers attempted to read a magazine while he waited to be checked by the doctor. The words were a blur as he flipped the pages. Frustrated, he tossed the magazine down, got up, and paced. All of a sudden the string that was wrapped around his paper gown slipped to the floor and exposed the front of his naked body. He hurried to retrieve it and tied it around his two hundred-fifty pound frame.

Bruce sat at the edge of the chair with his hands clasped and his eyes closed. Without warning the door banged open.

He jumped up, clinging to the front of his gown.

"Caught you napping," said Dr. Levin.

"I was just trying to relax."

"Is that why you're here…because you can't relax?"

Bruce sat down and looked directly at the doctor. "Yes…and I'm getting chest pains…then my heart pounds. Maybe I'm having a panic attack because of Mike's death. Is that possible?"

"Could be," Dr. Levin said. "Let's check you and find out."

He took Bruce's blood pressure and examined him. "Looks like there are a few potential problems to be concerned about."

"Are they serious?"

"Possibly, very serious."

Bruce sat up on the examining table. "What is it…what's wrong with me?"

"First of all, you have an irregular heart beat. I need to take tests to find out why."

Bruce grabbed his forehead and let out a deep sigh. "What could be causing that?"

"Several things," Dr. Levin said. "You're carrying too much weight which is not good for your heart. Also, your blood pressure is very high."

"How high?"

"190 over 100."

His eyes widened. "It's never been that high. Is that because of my weight, too?"

"That's one reason." The doctor peered at him over his glasses. "Heavy drinking could be another factor. How much do you drink a day?"

"Let me see, one or two bottles of whiskey and a couple of six-packs of beer lasts me two days."

Dr. Levin shook his head. "That's definitely too much. You must change your drinking and eating habits if you want to survive."

"I want to get better, Doc. Help me, please."

The doctor handed him a pamphlet. "This is a low fat diet plan. Make sure you follow it every day. Also, you've got to give up drinking. If you can't stop at once, cut down to two drinks a day until you can stop altogether."

"Anything else?"

"Start exercising daily. Begin with walking, short distances at first, then work toward high goals.

Bruce scowled and hung his head. "You didn't tell me any of this my last examination."

"That was two years ago. Looks like you've let yourself go since then."

The doctor put something in an envelope and handed it to him. "Here are a few pills to help your heart condition. Be sure to take one tonight after dinner and one before you go to bed. Take the other two pills tomorrow about the same time. Come back here after the funeral service on Monday. Skip breakfast that day because I'm going to run tests on your heart."

Dr. Levin looked at his patient. "That's a lot of instructions. Any questions?"

Bruce's eyes were misty. "Yeah…am I going to make it?"

"It depends on how you take care of yourself."

"I'm going to work hard at it." He shook the doctor's hand. "Thanks for the help, Doc, and for seeing me on a Saturday. You don't usually work weekends, do you?"

"Not as a rule." Dr. Levin smiled. "But I'm always happy to help a congressman when he needs me."

Bruce got dressed and combed his silver hair straight back. He frowned when he viewed himself in the mirror. His fingers traveled over every line on his face. After these last two days, he seemed to have grown older than his sixty-two years.

The ride home in his sleek, metallic-gray Lincoln Continental felt like an eternity. Bruce thought about his wife who had been dead three years. She had taken excellent care of him when she was alive. The visit to Dr. Levin's office made him aware of how he had neglected himself since her death.

The rest of his family, his two children and four grandchildren, lived in Minnesota. As their faces flashed before him, he was overcome with a strong urge to touch and hug them.

A few minutes later he dashed into his house and dialed the phone. "Hi, son. It's so good to hear your voice."

After talking with all the children, plans were made for a visit in the near future.

Bruce took the medication as Dr. Levin instructed and fell into a deep sleep both nights. He dragged himself out of bed early Monday morning and got ready to meet his friends at the funeral. He felt lightheaded while he drove to his destination. He concluded that it could be due to the stress of Mike's death.

A minister conducted the services followed by a eulogy by Bruce. "Mike Ryan was an honorable man...loyal to the country, his family, and his friends. We are all going to miss Mike's smiling face and his dedicated service in congress. Let's pray that the Lord is taking good care of him."

Bruce attempted to continue but the words stuck in his throat while tears streamed down his face. Mike's wife and young son embraced and cried. Everyone said good-bye to Mike and left the room.

All the members of the Aces High Club carried the casket down the steps and toward the limousine. Suddenly, Bruce gasped and collapsed to the ground, inches away from the car. The others put the casket down and yelled for help. Dr. Levin pushed his way through the crowd and checked Bruce.

"Call an ambulance," said the doctor.

In a few minutes, an ambulance arrived and took Bruce to a local hospital.

Dr. Levin assisted the rest of the pallbearers when they lifted the casket into the limousine. The men's faces reflected horror while they rode in silence to the cemetery which was located on the outskirts of Washington D.C.

Brenner called the hospital after he arrived home. He shook his head, put down the receiver, and stared out the window.

"Well, what they say? Is Bruce all right?" asked Jennie.

Brenner hesitated. "No. He's dead."

"Oh, my God," said Jennie as she covered her mouth. "It's unbelievable...two deaths in less than a week."

"Makes you wonder if there will be a third one."

She walked over to her husband and embraced him. "I hope it's not you. I can't bear the thought of losing you."

"Don't worry." His lips brushed her forehead. "I intend to be around for a long time."

She smiled. "That's good news." Her smile turned to a frown. "But I think their deaths are suspicious."

"Nonsense. I'm sure Dr. Levin will satisfy your doubts when he gives the results of the autopsies."

"Maybe. Sometimes my imagination runs wild."

He nodded. "I am going to meet the guys at the club. Try to get some rest while I'm gone."

Jennie sighed. "Alone again."

Brenner frowned and hurried out the door. He reached the club in about fifteen minutes and found everyone sitting at their usual table.

"We all meet again," said Johnny.

"Yeah, but this time two are missing. What the hell's going on?" asked Chuck while his husky body quivered.

Raymond pushed his unruly brown hair off his forehead and scowled. "First Mike, then Bruce. Kind of scary, don't you think?"

"Not really," Peter said. "I am sure it is just a coincidence."

"I agree," said Brenner.

"Maybe one of us will be next," Johnny said.

Chuck stood up. "Let's all try to remain calm until we hear the results of the autopsies." He went to the bar and returned with drinks for everyone.

"Chuck is right," said Johnny. "In fact, let's change the subject."

Raymond took a swig of his drink. "Great idea. I wonder who will be running for president? Has anyone heard any names?"

Chuck stared at Brenner. "I hear you've got an interest in running. Any truth in the rumor?"

Brenner blushed. "As a matter of fact, yes. I plan to run as an independent. What do you think?"

Johnny shook his head. "It's impossible for an independent to win."

"Nobody has ever done it before," said Raymond. "You'll have a better chance running as a democrat, the party that has kept you in office."

"I've done some polling on my own and I believe the country is ready for an independent president. I know I can win," smiled Brenner. "But I need a lot of help with the campaign. Any volunteers?"

"O.K. You can count on me," Johnny said.

"Me, too," said Raymond. "We certainly need a change."

Chuck put his fist in the air. "I'm behind you 100%."

The others followed and volunteered their services.

Johnny got up and ran his fingers through his black hair. "That's enough damn talking for one night. I'm beat…let's hit the road."

"Yeah, you're right," said Chuck.

Brenner got home just before midnight and was relieved to find Jennie in a sound sleep.

Tonight he won the support of his political friends, but realized that it was even more essential to have Jennie by his side during his campaign for president.

To find a way to satisfy her sexually was critical.

Chapter Three

The Aces High poker players were meeting for the first time in two weeks.

Tonight two new members sat in Mike's and Bruce's favorite chairs.

One of the men, Dr. Claude Levin, smiled at all the familiar faces and sat down in Mike's vacant chair. His disheveled black hair hung to his shoulders while dark shadows were visible under his somber brown eyes.

"Welcome aboard, Dr. Levin," said Johnny.

"I'm happy to be here, but please don't be so formal. Call me Claude."

Johnny stared him. "You look very pale and tired. Are you feeling all right?"

He shrugged his shoulders. "I'm a little beat from working long hours on those autopsies. But otherwise, I'm fine."

Chuck sipped his brandy. "Any results of the autopsies?"

Claude nodded. "Mike was diabetic and died of insulin shock. It may have been caused by his skipping a meal."

"What about Bruce?" asked Johnny.

"Heart attack. He neglected his body for years. By the time he came to me for help, it was too late."

Peter said, "So they both died of natural causes."

"Definitely," Claude said.

Brenner smiled. "Good job, Doc. Your report is such a relief."

A deep frown appeared on Johnny's face. "Maybe. But that doesn't stop one of us from dropping dead."

"The future is always uncertain," Claude said. "But chances for a longer life are better when you take good care of your body."

Brenner addressed Corey. "Honestly, we're not ignoring you, just catching up on some news."

"I understand."

"Your name is Corey Brown and this is your first year as a congressman, right?"

"Yes, sir."

Brenner yelled. "Hey guys! We've got a gentleman here. He called me sir."

Corey clasped his hands while his eyes were downcast.

Brenner slapped him gently on the back. "I was only kidding. It really felt good to be called sir." He stared him. "By the way, how old are you?"

"Thirty."

Brenner inspected Corey's physique. "And in great shape, I might add. Any tips for us old men on what we can do to look that good?"

Corey laughed. "You can come jogging with me every day. That's a start."

"I'll try it if you help with my cause," said Brenner.

"What cause?"

"I'll be campaigning for president soon and I'll need a lot of help. Can I count on your support?"

"Wow! I didn't know that you were running for president," Corey said. "Yes. I would love to help. When do you want me to start?"

"Soon." Brenner shook his hand and grinned. "It's great having you aboard, kid."

Chuck said, "What a lucky man. You're the youngest in the group and you'll soon be working for a possible future president."

"Amazing," beamed Corey.

Johnny pounded the table. "Hey! Enough damn business already. Let's play cards."

They played poker until almost midnight before the game broke up.

Brenner did not go straight home. Instead, he pulled up in the back of a dilapidated hotel and parked in the darkest section. After a quick glance around the area, he hurried inside. Brenner got into a dimly lit elevator with gray paint peeling off the walls, and male and female names scribbled on them. He stopped at the eighth floor, approached one of the rooms, and with a quick turn of a key, dashed inside.

Beads of sweat formed on Brenner's forehead as he ripped off his clothes and climbed into the bed.

"Bunny, oh, Bunny. It's been too long. I want you so bad."

He and his lover embraced and kissed with passion. All of the tension that he felt earlier was released during their wild sexual encounter. Satisfied, they collapsed like rag dolls and clung to each other.

Brenner glanced at his watch and jumped up. "Damn! It's late. I've got to get home."

"Don't stay away so long," said Bunny. "Let's meet sooner next time."

"We will, I promise."

Bunny covered his face with kisses. "I love your magnificent face."

Brenner gave Bunny one last tender kiss. "And I love you more than anyone in the world."

He showered, dressed quickly, and rushed out the door.

On his way home, Brenner reflected on the days when he was growing up. He was raised in a small mid-western town by his father, a minister, and his mother, an English teacher in the local high school.

Family loyalty and high morals were of the utmost importance, or it seemed, until that unforgettable night when Brenner was ten years old.

His mother was away for the weekend visiting relatives. On Friday Brenner returned home just after dark from baseball practice. While searching for his father throughout the house, he opened his parents' bedroom door and froze in place. Two nude bodies were moving on the bed. In horror, he recognized his

9

father fondling a young man who was in his early teens. Brenner muffled an outcry and ran out of the house. His heart raced as he ran faster around the town until he finally collapsed near a pond. Lying on his back, he looked up at the stars and felt like a dot in the universe. The awful scene he just witnessed played over and over in his mind. Although he was confused about what they were doing, it appeared that his father and the young boy enjoyed it.

His head swirled with so many questions and no one to turn to for answers.

Dawn was breaking when Brenner entered the house and tiptoed toward his room.

Suddenly his father jumped up from the couch. "Where the hell have you been? You've been gone all night."

"Walking around town."

"Do you know how dangerous it is to walk at night? Someone could have kidnapped you. Why were so foolish?"

Brenner's eyes shifted from his. "I had a lot on my mind."

His father pointed to a chair. "Sit down. We've got to talk."

Brenner obeyed and hung his head.

His father cleared his throat. "I saw you standing in my bedroom doorway last night. Did that upset you?"

"Yes, sir."

"Do you know what we were doing?"

"No, sir."

With a deep sigh his father said, "Believe me, it was nothing. We were just playing."

Brenner frowned and nodded.

"Son, even though nothing bad happened, I want you to forget about what you saw last night," his father said. "People will take it wrong. Understand?"

"Yes, sir."

His father stared at him. "Promise me you won't tell anyone, especially your mother. This is our secret."

Brenner's lower lip quivered. "I promise."

After that episode, every time he saw his father with a young man, he wondered if they were going to play his game.

In order to improve his self-image, Brenner worked diligently in high school, then college, resulting in exceptional performances in scholastic activities and sports.

During those years Brenner was confused about his feelings for girls and boys. He was terrified to be like his father toward males, and he was insecure regarding females.

When he met Jennie Cooper his sophomore year in college he experienced new feelings and thought he was in love. They married two years later and have remained married for twenty years. They had no children.

10

Brenner felt guilty about Bunny and also that Jennie failed to arouse him. In the earlier years he could fake his inability to get excited with her. Now it was difficult to pretend to be aroused. He realized that Jennie must never find out about his lover for one vital reason…his career would be over. He'd have to be very careful.

Bunny was so sensuous, sexy, and irresistible. All the frustrations of the day disappeared when they were together. Physically, he felt fulfilled, compared to Jennie when he attempted to make love to her and felt nothing.

No way could he give up Bunny.

Brenner hoped Jennie was sleeping when he arrived home. The key clicked in the lock and he walked softly into the house. He saw a light in the den, looked inside, and discovered Jennie lying on the couch.

She leaped up and glanced at her watch. "It's three in the morning. Where have you been?"

"We had some business to attend to after the poker game."

"What kind of business…woman business?"

Brenner shook his head. "No, no woman, believe me."

Jennie pushed the hair off her face. "Then why are you so late?'

"We were making plans for my campaign for president."

"So, you decided to run after all. Why didn't you tell me?"

"I just did."

"When did you make this decision?"

"This week."

Jennie pouted. "Why didn't you discuss it with me?"

Brenner threw up his arms. "Enough questions. I'm worn out. Let's talk in the morning."

Jennie walked toward the bedroom. "You're right. Let's sleep on it."

When they got in bed, Jennie moved close to Brenner. She lightly massaged his body but failed to stimulate him.

He pushed her hand away. "Come on, Jennie. It's late."

"It's always late, isn't it? You never have time to satisfy me."

Brenner was silent as he edged to the far side of the bed.

Jennie jumped up, ran to the door, and slammed it behind her.

Once again she lay on the bed in the guestroom feeling lonely. When sleep wouldn't come, she leaped up and pulled out the bureau drawer. Her hands clasped the full bottle of whiskey. The bottle was half full when she placed it back under some clothes. After reading a few pages of an enticing romantic novel, she closed her eyes and visualized the amorous man in the book lying beside her. He brushed his lips tenderly over her body then made love to her, causing her to tingle all over.

As she started to fall asleep, Jennie wondered how long a fantasy man could satisfy her.

The sun shone through the blinds and across Brenner's eyes. He reached for Jennie and realized that she had not returned to bed. Guilt overwhelmed him because of his inability to make love to her. He showered, dressed, and headed for the kitchen.

Jennie sauntered into the kitchen fifteen minutes later. She rubbed her eyes and stretched. "Something smells good in here. What's cooking?'

"Ham and cheese omelet, country sausage, and biscuits."

Jennie was wide-eyed. "You're cooking breakfast? You never do that. Where's Martha?"

"I gave her the day off."

Jennie shook her head. "Why are you doing this?"

"To make up for the way I treated you last night."

Jennie walked next to him. "I'm the one who should apologize to you. I accused you of being with another woman while you were with the guys discussing your campaign."

She put her arms around his neck and gazed at him. "Sorry for acting like a big fool."

His eyes shifted from hers while he gently broke away from her embrace. "The omelet is ready to burn. I need to flip it."

Minutes later they were sitting across from each other and enjoying breakfast and coffee.

"M-m-m-m...this is scrumptious," Jennie said. "You're a terrific cook. What else are you hiding from me?"

Brenner blushed. "Nothing."

Jennie laughed. "I thought you had some more hidden talents."

He shook his head. "Not that I'm aware of."

Jennie cleared the table, rinsed off the dishes, and put them in the dishwasher. She turned to Brenner. "Thanks again for the wonderful breakfast."

"It was nothing...just a couple of eggs."

"But everything was tasty."

"This is only the beginning," Brenner said.

"What do you mean?"

"After we get dressed, I thought we'd go to the mall, shop, take in a movie, whatever you feel like doing. How does that sound?"

"Terrific...but I can't believe it. We haven't done so many things in one day since before we got married."

Brenner took her hand. "Since Mike and Bruce died, I've become aware of how short life is. We have to enjoy each other while we can."

"How true."

"Then get dressed. It's Saturday...let's have some fun."

Jennie rummaged through her closet to find an outfit that would be appropriate for their plans for the day. She tried on a few dresses and picked one that accentuated her emerald-green eyes. A view of herself in her floor-length mirror assured Jennie that she made the right choice with her jade-green dress because it was loose enough to hide the extra pounds she had put on lately. She applied blush to her cheeks to brighten her pale face, then added a softer lipstick. Several squirts of hair spray helped her stubborn auburn hair fall into place.

For the most part, the woman looking back at her appeared okay and was ready for an adventurous day.

A hand touched her shoulder. "I'm a lucky man. I'm going out with the best looking woman in Alexandria."

Jennie smiled while he assisted with her coat. "You're trying to make me feel good, and it's working. Thanks." She took his arm. "You look quite handsome yourself, dear."

Brenner wore off-white slacks and a navy blazer that enhanced his deep blue eyes. His body was in good shape, except for his belly that had grown noticeably larger the past two years.

They clasped hands and walked into the car. Brenner started the wipers to clear the large snowflakes that were falling on the windshield.

"We better not be getting a snowstorm," Brenner said.

"This will probably pass. The paper predicted a good day."

"Hope you're right."

They reached the mall in ten minutes and found a parking place in front of the entrance. "What luck," said Brenner.

After browsing through most of the stores without buying a thing, Brenner said, "How about a new dress?"

"I could use one. All my dresses are too tight."

They walked into a store that featured women's apparel and Brenner patiently watched his wife try on about a dozen dresses. At last she chose a black dress that concealed her added weight.

Brenner whistled when she modeled it for him.

A shop for men's clothes was next door. It took Brenner ten minutes to decide on a pair of slacks, a jacket, and a matching tie.

"Wish I could shop that fast," Jennie said.

"It's a guy thing," laughed Brenner. "Need anything else?"

"One more item."

They stopped at a bookstore. Jennie skimmed the books and purchased the latest novel by one of her favorite authors.

"Let me guess what kind of book you bought," Brenner shifted his eyes upward. "A romantic, sexy novel."

"Not this time. It's a mystery story for a change, about people who die suddenly, the way Mike and Bruce did."

Deep lines appeared on Brenner's forehead. "Don't get any weird ideas. That book is only fiction."

13

"I know," Jennie said. "So why are you so upset?"

Brenner let out a deep sigh. "I'm not upset." He reached for her hand. "We have an hour to kill before the movie starts. How about a bite to eat?"

"Just something small."

They stopped at the Country Café and had cheeseburgers and chocolate milkshakes.

While she sampled her milkshake, Jennie viewed the room and the tables that were decorated in red and white plaid tablecloths. "This atmosphere reminds me of our first date. Remember?"

Brenner smiled. "Yes. What do you remember most?"

"That it was great to be young and in love."

Brenner blushed and stood up. "The movie's about to start. We'd better hurry."

They sat down near the front of the theatre. Brenner put his arm around his wife. "Are you enjoying yourself?"

She rested her head on his shoulder. "Oh, yes. And you remembered I love romantic movies." Jennie sighed. "The day has been wonderful so far."

"You haven't seen anything yet." Brenner took her hand and brushed his lips across it. Her body quivered a little.

When they left the mall, Jennie fastened the top buttons on her coat, and Brenner wrapped a scarf around his neck.

"We only got a brush of snow, like you predicted, but it's chillier," Brenner said as he started the car.

"Good cuddle weather," said Jennie while she moved alongside her husband.

They found a place with a red neon sign flashing steak...shrimp...lobster.

"This meet your approval?" asked Brenner.

"You're taking me out two times in one day. How come?"

"I want to make you happy. Now do you want me to stop here or somewhere else?"

"Let's try this place."

After their appetites were satisfied, they went into the lounge. A band played while couples danced.

Brenner took Jennie's hand. "How about a dance pretty lady?"

"It's been a long time. I don't know if I remember how to dance."

"Nonsense...you'll do fine."

He guided her to the dance floor and held her close as they swayed in rhythm to the music. While twirling fast around a corner, Jennie lost her balance and stepped on Brenner's foot.

Her face turned red. "Sorry. Are you all right?"

He held his breath and winced. "I'm fine."

Brenner limped off the dance floor and sat down.

"Told you I couldn't dance," Jennie said.

"You did great, until you landed on my foot."

Her eyes were downcast. "Guess we won't go dancing again."

"Of course we'll go again and when we do, we'll do better."

Jennie pushed her chair back. "Can we go now? I'm getting tired."

"Sure," Brenner said. "We've done a lot in one day."

On the way home, Jennie put her head back. "Thanks for the wonderful evening, except for stepping on your foot."

"You're too hard on yourself. Forget it, please."

"Sorry, I won't mention it again. I don't want to spoil the fabulous day we shared," said Jennie. "Thanks for everything."

"You are definitely worth it. "Brenner squeezed her hand. "There will be more times like this. I promise." He kissed her hand.

Jennie felt some slight flutters inside her.

When they got home, Brenner was the first one in bed. Jennie, dressed in a white lacy negligee, climbed into bed.

"Come over here," her husband said. He put his arm around her and pulled her next to him.

His hand moved lightly down her body. "What do you have on?"

"A negligee. Don't you like it?"

"Yes, but I like you better with it off." He slipped it over her head and started fondling her body.

He paused. "Why are you so tense?"

"I'm afraid."

"Of what?"

Jennie took a deep breath. "Afraid we'll fail."

"No way. We're going to make it this time." Brenner ran his tongue slowly over Jennie's body while he caressed her. When Jennie started to get excited, he attempted to make love to her, failed, and rolled over in disgust.

"Told you so," Jennie said.

"Sorry."

"Don't you love me anymore?" asked Jennie.

"Of course I do. Maybe it's because I've had a lot on my mind lately, or I could be trying too hard to make love to you."

She turned away from him. "And maybe you've got another woman."

"There's no other woman, I swear."

"You haven't proven it to me."

"You've got to trust me."

Jennie started to cry. "How can I trust you when you can't make love to me? There has to be someone else."

She got up, went into the guestroom, and released more tears. Then she entered her fantasy world where a sensuous man made love to her until the hurt vanished.

While Jennie was eating breakfast the following morning, Martha handed her an envelope. "Mr. Sands told me to give this to you. He said it was important." She grinned. "I bet it's a love letter."

"Did you peek at it?"

"Oh no, ma'am, I'd never do that." She started to walk away.

"Wait," Jennie said.

Martha brushed some gray hair back to the bun in back of her head, and crossed her hands over her round plump belly.

Jennie ripped open the envelope and pulled out a note:

'Sorry about last night. Please give me a chance to make it up to you. How about dinner and dancing tonight? I'll call you later. Love, Brenner.'

She looked up at Martha. "Not exactly a love letter. But he did ask me out for dinner tonight. Should I go?"

"Yes, go." Her bright blue eyes glanced upward. "It could be a romantic evening."

Jennie laughed. "In that case, my answer is yes."

Because of a light schedule that day, Brenner was able to leave early. He called his wife just before he left and was home about twenty-five minutes later.

When Brenner walked in the house, Jennie greeted him with a kiss. "You kept your word."

"Did you doubt me?"

"A little."

Brenner held her at arm's length. "You look too good to stay home."

"Thanks."

Jennie wore her new black dress, which made her appear ten pounds lighter. Gold jewelry completed her neat appearance.

Brenner showered then changed into his new gray jacket and blue slacks.

Jennie touched the soft brown curls, lightly streaked with gray, that brushed his forehead. "You're rather sexy-looking for your age." With her head held high, she took his arm.

He smiled and led her to the car. They arrived at a restaurant that was located on the remote part of town. Inside, crystal chandeliers were suspended from the ceiling and exotic plants hung alongside the walls.

"We've never been here before," Jennie said. "It's beautiful."

"Peter suggested it to me. He and Peggy come here once in a while. He said the food is great."

Jennie ordered a lobster and Brenner prime rib.

"This is luscious," Jennie said.

"Try some of mine. It melts in your mouth." Brenner and Jennie sampled each other's plates.

A few minutes later Jennie put down her fork and looked at her husband. "I've been doing a lot of thinking lately."

"Oh? Good thoughts, I hope."

"I think so…I want to have a baby."

Brenner almost choked on his beef. "You know we can't have children. We had tests and was told I'm sterile, remember?"

"I realize that. I mean, adopt. Let's adopt a baby."

He shook his head. "We're too old to adopt."

"No we aren't. My Uncle Fred and Aunt Sally were fifty years old when they adopted Alice."

Brenner twisted his napkin while his face turned crimson. "Well, I'm too busy to help take care of a baby."

Jennie nodded. "You're right. You're too busy, even for me. I'm left alone for many hours. I want a baby to love and take care of…one to fill those hours. Please say yes."

"Let's talk about this after the campaign," Brenner said. "You'll have plenty to do once we start. You won't have time for a baby."

She shrugged her shoulders. "You're running, not me."

"I need your support," Brenner said. "Are you willing to help?"

Jennie's eyes lowered. "I'm not sure."

Brenner held her hands and stared at her. "Wouldn't you love to be First Lady?"

She smiled. "First Lady. That does sound wonderful."

"Then you'll help?"

"All right. But can we try for a baby once the campaign is over?"

Brenner sighed. "Yes, my dear, we'll talk about it then. Now let's finish this delicious food."

After dinner they made their way into the lounge to have a couple of drinks and listen to the band. Brenner took his wife's hand and led her to the dance floor. Jennie stumbled a little during a slow song.

"Relax. You're doing fine," Brenner said.

"Then why are those people in front laughing at me?"

"They're not laughing at you, but maybe they are telling each other jokes."

Jennie struggled through the rest of the dance and headed toward their table.

"Wait," said Brenner. "A jazz song just started."

"What makes you think I can dance to that?"

"It was one of your favorite songs when we were younger. Just concentrate and it'll come back to you."

Jennie reluctantly followed her husband back to the dance floor. Gradually she felt the rhythm and started moving to the jazz music. A few times she tripped over own feet but, for the most part, she danced fairly well.

The song ended and they walked back to their table.

"Lady, you were great."

She laughed. "I wouldn't call it great, but at least I didn't step on your feet this time."

Brenner glanced at his watch. "I hate to say this but we really should be going. It's almost midnight."

"Oh, well. All good things must come to an end, I guess."

"For tonight anyway. We'll do it again soon."

On the way home, Jennie snuggled beside her husband and put her head on his shoulder. "Thanks for tonight. I loved every minute of it."

"I enjoy pleasing you."

A full moon shone brightly to light their way home.

Jennie, dressed in a teddy, was the first one in bed. Brenner slid over to her and gathered her in his arms. He slipped off the teddy, kissed her tenderly, and ran his tongue over her body. She groaned and pulled him closer. He visualized Bunny's enticing body, became aroused, and, at last, was able to make love to Jennie. In minutes, she was satisfied and fell into a deep sleep.

Brenner wondered if tonight would help keep Jennie loyal to him during his campaign for president.

He knew it would take more than one night to keep her happy. It was essential to find a way to continue satisfying her.

Chapter Four

"Why don't we have a dinner party for the campaign workers and their wives, sort of a get acquainted gathering?" asked Brenner while he sipped his coffee the next morning.

Jennie peered at him from across the table. "I don't know how to arrange that kind of event."

"Call Peter's wife, Peggy. She might be willing to help. That would give you a chance to get to know her better."

She nodded. "I'll ask her to lunch. Maybe we'll come up with some good ideas."

"That's my girl." He got up and bent down to kiss her. She pulled his head down and whispered in his ear. "Last night was great. Got time for seconds?"

Brenner blushed and glanced at his watch. "I'll have to take a rain check. I've got to go or I'll be late for work."

He kissed her and hurried to his car.

After pouring another cup of coffee, Jennie reflected on the night before, making love to her husband, reaching her climax, and feeling warm all over. Chills traveled up and down her spine as she thought about the ecstasy she experienced. She hoped there would be many nights like that to reminisce on in the future.

Jennie prepared a hot bubble bath and lay in it for about an hour while she read a romantic novel.

She called Peggy a couple of hours later and arranged to meet her for lunch.

Just before noon Jennie entered Golden City Restaurant, spotted Peggy, and sat down opposite her.

Peggy's blue-green eyes twinkled as she leaned forward. "Got some good gossip to tell me?"

Jennie grinned. "Sorry...no gossip today. The reason I asked you to meet me is to talk about a dinner party."

"What dinner party?"

"For the ones who are working on Brenner's campaign." She frowned. "He wants me to make the arrangements, and I'm lost on how to do it."

"And you want me to organize this party?"

"Not exactly. I'm asking you to help me with it. You've entertained a lot and know what to do." Jennie touched her arm. "Please help me."

Peggy smiled. "Since my husband will be Brenner's running mate, I guess I should help."

A waitress approached their table. "Are you ready to order, ladies?"

"Bring us two martinis for now," Jennie said.

After the waitress walked away, she stared at Peggy. "Peter's going to be Brenner's running mate? He didn't tell me."

"Maybe it's because he won't announce it until the campaign is under way, or maybe he forgot."

"Brenner just recently told me about his intentions to run. Looks like I'm the last to anything." She finished her martini and ordered another one.

"Don't take it personally," said Peggy. "Men don't think like women. It was probably an oversight."

"Maybe you're right." She motioned for the waitress and ordered two Greek salads.

"Now," Jennie said. "Where do we start with this party?"

"First of all, it should be informal so everyone will be relaxed."

"I agree."

Peggy sipped her drink. "I recommend Richardos for catering. They're excellent."

"Can you go there with me and help plan the menu?"

Peggy nodded. "When do you want this get together?"

"A week from Saturday."

"Then we'd better get over to Ricardos tomorrow. They're usually very busy. I'm not sure if they can do it on such short notice, but we can ask."

The waitress brought the check and laid it on table. Jennie paid the bill and handed the waitress a ten dollar tip.

"Thank you, ladies." She smiled while she slipped the money into her pocket.

When they were walking toward their cars, Peggy said, "How about stopping by my house to talk about what we've got to do?"

"Sounds great."

They drove in separate cars and arrived at Peggy's house in twenty minutes. Peggy led Jennie into the den where she fixed two more drinks. Every time the women attempted to discuss the upcoming affair, they giggled and covered their mouths.

"Hell with that party for now." Peggy swept some strands of strawberry-blonde hair from her eyes. "Let's talk about fun things."

Jennie snickered. "Sex is fun. You getting enough?"

"Not as much as I need."

"Isn't Peter good in bed?"

Peggy shrugged her shoulders and laughed. "Depends on what you call good. We don't have sex often enough to satisfy me. He's either too busy with his job, or too tired."

"The same for us. Brenner and I got together for the first time in months the other night. It was great but I wonder when it will happen again."

"I'm thinking of having an affair, find someone really hot to release my passions to," Peggy said.

"You'd better find another way to cool your desires. You can't take a chance now that Peter's going to be Brenner's running mate. Why don't you try what I do?"

"What's that?"

"I turn to my fantasy man when I get frustrated."

Peggy gagged on her drink then chuckled. "Fantasy man? How can a fantasy man relieve your tensions?"

"Believe me, he does. Just imagine every bit of a sex scene with a hunk." Jennie smirked. "And whatever else satisfies you."

Peggy giggled. "I'll try it the next time I'm frustrated. I'll let you know how it turns out."

"I works for me." Jennie got up to use the bathroom. Her body swayed when she attempted to walk. "I think I'm getting tipsy."

"You look good to me," Peggy said.

Peter got home about an hour later and found both women asleep in their chairs. He walked up to Peggy and shook her.

She opened her eyes. "What's the matter?"

"That's what I want to know. Why are you both sleeping here?"

"Because we're tired?"

Peter went to the bar and picked up the empty whiskey bottle and sniffed the two glasses next to it.

"Looks like you girls are smashed."

Peggy snickered. "Who, us? No way."

Jennie stretched and stood up. "This room's moving." She collapsed backwards into the chair.

"Does Brenner know you're here?" Peter asked.

Jennie shook her head. "I've got to get home."

"You're not driving in that condition. I'll take you home," said Peter. He got Jennie's belongings and led her out the door. She staggered, grabbed his arm, and followed him into the car.

"What were you two doing today?"

"I don't remember," said Jennie as she edged closer to Peter.

She touched his cheek. "What a strong-looking face." Her hand moved lightly down his leg. "You're so lean, baby...all over." She continued downward until her hand stopped between his legs. "This is what I want," she moaned.

He grabbed her hand. "You don't know what you're doing. You're drunk."

"I want to get laid."

"You'll be home in a few minutes. Brenner will take care of you."

21

"He doesn't know how to take care of me. But I bet you could," said Jennie as she messaged his leg.

Peter pulled into her driveway. "You're home. Tomorrow you won't remember a word you said."

He opened the door and put out his hand. Jennie took it and pulled herself out of the car. She stood up, pressed herself against his body, and leaned her head on his chest. "Kiss me."

He broke away and led her toward the house.

"You are going to make love to me someday, just wait and see," Jennie said.

"Stop talking crazy." Peter stopped in front of the door and held out his hand. "Give me your key."

Jennie searched in her purse. "Damn! I can't find it."

"Never mind." Peter rang the doorbell. The door opened and Brenner gaped at them. "I was worried about you, Jennie. Where have you been?"

"Our wives celebrated a little bit too much today," Peter said while he and Jennie walked into the house.

"Hi, sweetie. I've missed you." Jennie threw her arms around his neck and kissed him.

He gently pushed her away. "You and Peggy were supposed to plan the campaign party."

"Oh, we did. We've got it al-l-l-l-l-l planned."

Brenner looked at Peter. "What was she drinking?"

"Martinis and whiskey."

He shook his head. "I've never seen her like this. Can you stay a few minutes until I get her to bed?'

"I'd better not. I've got to get back home and take care of my wife." Peter ran out the door.

Brenner led Jennie to their bedroom, undressed her, and put her in bed. He felt frustrated with her behavior, but relieved that he would not have to give excuses for not making love to her.

Jennie woke up about nine o'clock the next day with an upset stomach and a throbbing head. After a piece of toast and a cup of black coffee, her head started to clear. She reached for the phone.

"Peggy. What the hell hit me?"

"I guess you had too many martinis. We'll have to cool it from now on."

"Are you up to going to Ricardos today?" asked Jennie.

"Yes, I'll meet you in an hour."

Peggy picked up Jennie and headed for the caterers.

"I can't remember anything after getting to your house, do you?" Jennie asked.

"Not much."

They met with Ricardo and planned a menu for the get together. Another stop was made to buy liquor and soda.

"What's next?"

"Have you invited the guests yet?" asked Peggy.

"No. Do I need invitations?"

"No time for that. You'll have to call them."

Peggy pulled in back of Golden City Restaurant. "Let's discuss this over lunch.

Jennie ordered a martini while they waited for their sandwiches. She took out two pieces of paper, wrote down names on each, and handed one paper to Peggy. "I've divided the list of the guests in half. Could you call these names and I'll take care of the rest?"

"No problem," Peggy said as she tasted her coke.

Jennie devoured the rest of her martini and motioned to the waitress for another.

"I thought we were going to cool it?"

"I'm only having a couple of drinks to unwind. Come on, have one with me."

"No thanks. I promised Peter I'd be good today."

"Do you always listen to your husband?"

"When he makes sense."

Jennie downed her drink. "I'll be good, too. That's my last one for today."

When they finished eating, Peggy reached for the check.

Jennie grabbed it away from her. "Hey, I'm treating you."

"It's my turn to pay."

"Since you're helping me, I'll take care of it." Jennie stood up. "Time's flying. We'd better start calling people."

Peggy weaved in and out of traffic with caution on the way back to her house.

"Where are you going?" asked Jennie.

"Don't you remember?" You left your car at my house last night. Peter drove you home."

Jennie scowled. "I don't recall leaving my car at your place, or going home with Peter."

"Didn't you notice your car missing?"

"No."

"Boy, you were in worse shape than I realized."

In minutes, Peggy pulled alongside Jennie's car.

"Let me know how many are coming to the party from your list," said Jennie as got into her car.

She waved to Peggy and drove home.

Jennie took out her list and called a few people. Most were not home. She reached Dr. Levin at his office. He said he would talk to Amber, his fiancee, and call back with an answer. She contacted one more person, Nicole, the wife of Corey Brown, the young congressman and newest member of the poker club.

"I'd be delighted to come but I do have to check with Corey," said Nicole. "It shouldn't be a problem. By the way, could you call me Nikki?"

"Of course. I'm looking forward to meeting you, Nikki."

Jennie got in touch with the rest of the guests after dinner. She was thrilled with the results.

Her last call for the night was to Peggy. "How did you make out?"

"Just fine. They're all coming. What about you?"

"Everyone on my list said yes. Isn't that great? That's fourteen, counting us. Do you think we ordered enough food?"

"Plenty," said Peggy.

"One more thing," Jennie said. "Do you have a good dress?"

"Not one I'd want to wear. Want to go shopping for one?"

"Great idea. We deserve a new dress after all our hard work."

Jennie picked up Peggy about ten in the morning. They went to a near by mall and tried on dresses in all the stores, but found nothing they liked. Frustrated and exhausted, the women returned to the first shop they went to.

After trying on three or four dresses, Peggy turned to Jennie. "Do you like this one?"

"I love it. The light blue color enhances your eyes and hair. And it fits like a glove."

"It doesn't make me look too fat?"

"Are you serious," laughed Jennie. "There's not an inch of fat on your whole body."

It took Jennie a little longer but she finally found a white dress she liked. They paid for the dresses and left.

On the way out of the mall, Jennie pointed to a restaurant, Cove Pub. "Let's stop here."

They ordered sub sandwiches and drinks.

Peggy twirled the glass slowly in her hand. "I shouldn't drink this."

"Don't be silly. One won't hurt you."

"Guess you're right."

Jennie lifted her glass. "To a job well done. Without you, I couldn't have arranged all this."

"It's been fun. I've enjoyed it."

After Jennie dropped Peggy off, she went home, poured herself a martini, and waited for her husband.

Brenner walked into the den about 6:30 in the evening and found the television blaring and Jennie asleep on the couch.

He nudged her. "Are you O.K.?"

Jennie jumped up. "I must've dozed off." She rubbed her eyes, swayed back and forth, and fell backwards on to the couch.

"You're drunk. What have you been drinking?"

Brenner picked up an empty container and sniffed it "Martinis again. You've got to slow down with that stuff."

"I'm fine. I just had a couple of drinks to relax. Arranging that party was stressful."

Brenner paced the floor, stopped, and glared at Jennie. "You can't drink like this again, understand? I'll never be able to run for president if they find out my wife's a lush."

Jennie lowered her eyes. "I won't drink again, I promise." She staggered toward him with open arms. "Give me a hug, please."

Brenner put his hands in front of him. "No! Don't you touch me." He turned away and hurried out the door.

He stopped at a small restaurant, had a cup of coffee, and made a phone call. "Can you get away for a while?"

With a pounding heart, Brenner lay on the bed in a motel room that was located on the outskirts of town. Soon he felt someone slide beside him.

"Oh, Bunny. You feel so good."

They embraced and made love until their bodies became weak.

Brenner entered the house a couple of hours later and found Jennie sleeping, fully clothed, on their bed. An empty glass with a strong aroma of whiskey was on a table beside the bed. Brenner walked carefully out of their room and into the guestroom. The scent and touch of Bunny lingered when he drifted into a deep sleep.

The next morning Brenner entered the kitchen and found Jennie holding a cup of coffee and crying.

"You're up early," Brenner said. "What's wrong? Is your hangover making you cry?"

"No, it's you. How come you didn't sleep with me last night?"

"You ticked me off," yelled Brenner. "Remember your promise, never to drink again? You couldn't last through one night, could you?"

Jennie wiped some tears and blew her nose. "You stormed out of the house and left me alone again. I was unhappy so I took a drink to feel better."

"I left because you broke your promise about drinking." Brenner shook his finger at her. "You've got to cut down on drinking, hear me?"

Jennie sighed. "I hear you. I'll do my best."

Brenner gulped down a cup of coffee, grabbed his coat, and spoke more gently to Jennie. "Why don't you join a health club? Maybe that will help you relax."

She shrugged her shoulders. "What I need is more sex."

"If you stay sober, maybe it will happen." Brenner dashed out the door.

Chapter Five

Brenner viewed his wife and whistled. "You look radiant, my dear."

"Good enough to be a hostess?"

"Oh, yes. Pretty enough to be a princess."

Jennie smiled and twirled in front of the mirror. The white dress seemed to cover the bulges adequately, while it extended half way past her knees. Her auburn hair swerved in soft curls to the top of her head, making her appear taller than her actual height, five-feet-five. Jennie stared at her reflection and realized that the special grooming she received from her hairdresser had paid off.

Brenner crept up behind her and softly kissed her neck. "Now can you picture yourself as the First Lady?"

"Oh, yes."

"If you stay away from the booze and keep this image, you'll make a fine First Lady. Do you think you can behave yourself tonight?"

Jennie's chin protruded as she spoke. "Of course."

The doorbell rang. Peggy and Peter were the first ones to arrive at the dinner party.

"You look very nice, Peggy," said Jennie.

"So do you, doesn't she Peter?"

Peter nodded. "You both look lovely."

The rest of the guests arrived in a short while. Everyone gathered around the bar, had drinks, talked, and laughed.

Jennie motioned to the bartender. "A martini, please."

"Change that to a coke," Brenner said.

She held up one finger. "Just one won't hurt me."

Brenner glared at her. "No. Not a drop."

Jennie reluctantly took the coke.

"Come with me," Brenner said. "I want you to meet some people." He led her to a couple across the room.

"Corey and Nikki Brown, this is my wife, Jennie."

"I'm happy you could make it," Jennie said.

"It's our pleasure," said Nikki. "This is a lovely party."

"Do you work outside the home?" asked Jennie.

Nikki's large dark eyes sparkled while she looked up at her husband. "Making Corey happy is my full time job."

Jennie glanced at Brenner. "Same here. That's the woman's job, I guess."

Brenner smirked and nodded.

"Corey, what do you think the role of the woman should be in the home?" asked Jennie.

He hesitated. "Whatever makes her happy."

27

"I like that. And I hear that you're going to help Brenner with the campaign?"

"Yes." Corey smiled. "I'm looking forward to it."

Jennie turned to Nikki. "Would you like to help, too?"

"I'd love to. What do you want me to do?"

"How about getting together for lunch sometime? We could talk about it then."

"Sounds great…call me."

Brenner interrupted them. "I wonder how the food's coming along. I think everyone's ready to eat."

"I'll check."

Jennie walked toward the kitchen, turned to see if Brenner was watching, and darted into the den. She poured herself a drink, downed it quickly, and went into the kitchen.

When Jennie returned, Brenner asked, "How long will it be before the food is ready?"

"About a half hour."

"Come on. There are more people I want you to meet."

He took her hand, and walked over to another couple.

"Good evening, Dr. Levin," Brenner said. "I hope you're having a good time."

"Yes. It's a delightful party."

Brenner said to Jennie, "This is Dr. Levin's fiancee, Amber."

"Pleased to meet you," Jennie said.

Amber, a thin woman with short black hair, smiled and shook her hand. "My pleasure, ma'am."

While they were socializing, the caterers appeared and arranged the food on a long table. A beautiful vase of multi-colored roses was placed in the center. Trays of finger sandwiches, a relish tray, a platter of roast beef, ham, turkey, and varied cheeses, fresh-baked rolls, a fruit tree with dip, and many splendid desserts, aligned the table. Everyone filled their plates and sat down.

Brenner stood up with a glass of champagne held high. "Here's to all of wonderful people who have agreed to work on my campaign. Thanks for coming."

They all raised their glasses. "To our future president."

Brenner smiled and motioned for them to start their dinner.

"This food's wonderful," said Dr. Levin.

"Exquisite," Amber said.

Brenner was engrossed in a conversation with Chuck Andrews and did not see his wife fill her glass several times with champagne. He turned to talk to Jennie and discovered she was gone. Brenner glanced around the room and saw her stumbling toward Peter, who was standing alone near the den. He excused himself from his friends and walked with long strides toward Jennie. By this time, she was whispering in Peter's ear, then laughing loudly. Brenner rushed to them.

"Sorry about this, Peter. Looks like my wife found the whiskey again."

"And the champagne," grinned Jennie.

Brenner took her arm. "Come with me. We need to talk."

"Can Peter come too? He's so cute." Jennie ran her fingers through his dark, wavy hair.

Peter's face turned crimson. "Some other time. I have to get back to the party." He dashed across the room and joined a group of men who were talking.

Brenner led Jennie into the den. He found an opened bottle of whiskey with an empty glass next to it. Jennie headed for the bottle and was stopped by her husband.

"Don't you dare have another drink."

She swayed toward Brenner and snuggled up to him. "I won't have to drink if you're nice to me."

"How can I be nice to you when you broke your promise and continue to drink?" He pushed her away. "Why, Jennie…why do you have to drink so much?"

"Because it makes me feel good."

"That's nonsense." He shook his finger at her. "You've got to quit drinking or you'll hurt my campaign. Understand?"

She closed her eyes and nodded.

Brenner's voice softened. I'll get help for you if you need it."

"I don't need help. I can stop on my own."

"Hope you're right." Brenner took her hand. "Let's go back. Our guests will be wondering where we are."

A member of the poker club, Johnny Ruben, met them when they walked back into the room. "Where have you guys been so long?"

"We were having a quickie, weren't we, dear?" Jennie giggled and winked at her husband.

Brenner's face turned red. "Don't talk like that."

"Sounds good to me," chuckled Johnny. "You're a lucky man, Brenner."

For the rest of the evening Brenner watched every move Jennie made. Even though she craved another drink, she had to settle for black coffee.

The party broke up about 1 a.m.

Everyone smiled and thanked the host and hostess as they were leaving.

When the door closed behind the last guest, Jennie let out a deep sigh. "The party was a success after all, wasn't it?"

"Yes, despite your drinking and acting foolish at times."

Jennie pouted. "I didn't act foolish. I was just having a good time."

"Sure...a good time," Brenner glared at his wife. "I'm warning you, if you can't stop on your own, I'll make arrangements for you to get help."

"I can do it. Trust me."

They undressed and climbed into bed. Brenner kissed her on the forehead and turned with his back to her. In minutes he fell into a deep sleep while Jennie stared into space. Her body ached for her husband's touch...for him to make passionate love to her. At that moment she craved intimacy more than a drink. Frustrated, she turned to her fantasy man for comfort.

Chapter Six

Jennie paused a few moments, took a deep breath, then yanked the door open. She walked up to a young woman who was seated at the desk.

"May I help you?"

"I'd like to join your health club," Jennie said.

"Follow me." The slim woman led her into a small room with a desk and two chairs. In a short while Jennie handed her a completed application and a check for $500.00.

They entered a large room with various kinds of exercise equipment. Men and women were using the machines. In another huge room there was an enormous swimming pool, a sauna and a whirlpool. Nearby an exercise class was about to begin.

"Is it too late for me to join that class?" Jennie asked.

"Not if you hurry."

She changed into shorts with a matching top and scampered to the end of the group. Soon she was gasping for air. Jennie finished the class at a slower rate of speed, showered, and put on her bathing suit. She jumped into the pool and felt invigorated when the cool water met her warm skin. After swimming a couple of laps, she felt something bump into her leg.

A man emerged suddenly. "Sorry. Did I hurt you?"

"No. You just startled me."

Wet, blond curls touched his forehead and a grin was visible on his youthful face. "Did you think I was a shark?"

Jennie laughed. "There better not be any sharks in here."

"If there are, I'll save you, pretty lady."

"Thank you. That's encouraging."

"I'd like to know who I'm saving. I'm Randy Karr, what's your name?"

Jennie hesitated. "Jean...Jean Golden."

"I haven't seen you here before. Are you new?'

"Yeah. It's my first time here."

Randy grinned. "For your initiation, I'll race you to the end of the pool and back. I'll let you start first. Go."

Jennie started swimming as fast as she could. When she reached about one-quarter of the distance, Randy began to swim with strong, overhand strokes. He was waiting for her when she reached the end of the pool.

"I guess I need a lot more practice," said Jennie.

Randy's eyes twinkled. "That means you'll have to come here more often."

"Looks that way."

"I'm going into the whirlpool," he said. "Want to join me?"

"O.K."

When he climbed out of the water Jennie gaped at his lean, muscular body. His skin-tight bathing suit outlined his appealing masculinity. Her heart raced while the blood rushed to her face. She quickly looked away.

Jennie sat opposite Randy in the whirlpool. She lay her head back and closed he eyes. Every bit of her body relaxed from the hot streams of water that ejected and swirled around her.

"Feels good, doesn't it?"

She sighed. "Fantastic."

Randy pointed to a room across from them. "That's the sauna. It's even better than this. We could go in there and no one would see us with the steamed windows. Want to try it?"

"Not today." She blushed and closed her eyes again.

He tapped Jennie's hand lightly. "Hey! Want to go for a drink instead?"

"No way. I'm too content to move."

Randy smirked. "If you stay in here any longer your skin will get wrinkled."

Jennie jumped up. "I'd better get out right away."

"Now are you ready for that drink?"

"All right, but only one, then I've got to go home."

"It's a deal." Randy stepped out of the hot tub and grabbed a towel. "Meet me in front in ten minutes."

Jennie took a cold shower, dressed, and hurried to the lobby. Her heart pounded as she walked toward Randy, who was a gorgeous sight in his tight jeans and tee shirt.

"Where are we going?" Jennie asked.

"There's a small place around the corner." He took her hand and led her to it. They entered the dimly lit bar and sat down in front of a small band that was playing soft rock music.

"What would you like to drink, beautiful lady?"

Blood rushed to her cheeks. "A coke, please."

"I'm sure you can do better than that." He ordered two beers.

Randy sipped his beer. "Are you married?"

Her eyes lowered. "Sort of."

"Sort of?"

"I'd rather not talk about it."

He reached for her hand. "O.K. Then let's dance."

Randy held her close with her head resting on his shoulders. Jennie's body tingled as they danced slowly to the music. She reflected on her fantasy man and discovered that Randy resembled him.

After a couple of hours of drinking and dancing, Randy whispered in Jennie's ear. "How would you like to come to my place?"

She looked at him. "Is your wife there?"

"No wife, just me. How about it?"

Jennie hesitated and gazed into his enticing blue eyes. "All right. But only for one drink then I must leave."

"Your wish is my command," said Randy.

His apartment was near by. When they walked inside, Jennie was convinced it was a bachelor's pad. His king-sized bed was not made; pictures on the walls displayed shapely women; and several dishes were in the sink. A stereo with high speakers and a large screened television barely fit in a small den.

"Excuse the mess," said Randy. "You know how bachelors are."

Jennie smiled. "I think it's rather cozy."

She sat on a barstool while he mixed two drinks.

Randy leaned on the bar and searched her eyes. "A pretty woman like you must be married."

"I told you that I don't want to talk about it."

"Is he mean to you? Is that why you don't want to talk about it?"

Jennie picked up her purse and headed toward the door. "I've got to go."

"Wait!" Randy grabbed her arm and coaxed her to sit down on the couch beside him. "I'm sorry. I shouldn't have said those things." He slipped his arm around her shoulder. "Let's enjoy each other."

He pulled her close and softly blew into her ear. Their lips met with a long kiss, causing Jennie to feel lightheaded and her heart to pound wildly. Randy's hand traveled to her breasts and gently caressed them.

Jennie pushed his hand away. "Don't, please."

"You know you want me, babe." Randy's tongue found her ear.

"I can't do this." She turned her head away. "I hardly know you."

"Then let's get better acquainted." His hand gently massaged her hard nipples.

Jennie's breathing became heavy while she felt tingling sensations all over her body. He kissed her again with passion and her control began to slip.

Randy stood up. "Come on. There's more room on my bed."

Jennie followed him into the bedroom and stopped.

The alluring young man motioned to her. "Lay down next to me. It's so soft and comfortable."

Her heart raced as she slid beside him. Randy caressed her body tenderly, followed by several fiery kisses. He ripped off his tee shirt, unzipped his pants, and pulled them and his briefs off his hair-roughened legs. He motioned for Jennie to do the same. With trembling hands she slipped off all her clothes. Jennie was in ecstasy as they made passionate love. Her needs were fulfilled more than she could envision, much more than with her fantasy man.

After they were both satisfied, they lay still with their arms around each other and his muscular legs entwined in hers.

All of a sudden Jennie jumped up and looked at her watch. "It's late. I've got to get home."

Randy pulled her near him. "Stay the night. I promise that the second time will be better than the first."

"I'd love to, honest. But I must leave."

"I know, your husband."

Jennie nodded, dressed, and headed for the door.

"Hey, Jean. When will I see you again?"

She paused and stared at him. "I don't think we should see each other again."

Randy sat up. "Why not? Didn't you enjoy being with me?"

"Too much." Her lips quivered. "Be realistic. I'm too old for you. I think you should date a younger woman."

"Nonsense. I prefer older women because they know how to please a man," Randy said. "And you sure know how to please me, babe. So, when do we meet again?"

"You win, as usual," sighed Jennie. "I'll meet you at the spa, day after tomorrow." She waved and dashed out the door.

Jennie turned the key in the lock with care and tiptoed into the house. A figure jumped off the couch and stood before her. She gasped then recognized Brenner, who peered at her with blood shot eyes while he pushed back his disheveled hair.

"Where the hell have you been? It's two in the morning."

"I joined a health spa like you suggested."

Brenner glared at her. "They stay open all night?"

Jennie's eyes shifted from his. "I met a woman, Francie, there. We went to her house for a while and talked. You know how women like to talk."

"You were with a woman all this time?" His eyes shifted upward. "You actually expect me to believe that story?"

Jennie's face turned red. "What about the times you stayed out late, like three in the morning? You expected me to believe your explanations."

"Yeah, you're right. Sorry for giving you such a hard time but I was worried about you." He put his arms around her. "Let's go to bed."

When they got into bed Brenner moved beside Jennie and started caressing her body. She pushed his hand away and faced the wall.

"Not tonight. I'm beat."

Brenner lay awake wondering who Jennie was with tonight, perhaps another man. This was the first time that she had rejected him. A twinge of jealousy engulfed him as he drifted off to sleep.

Jennie continued to go to the spa about four times a week. After she exercised and swam several laps, Randy met her and took her to his apartment where they made love. Every meeting seemed to be more satisfying. Jennie hoped the bliss that she experienced would never end.

Brenner questioned her but she would not admit to her affair.

One evening Jennie went to the spa and discovered that Randy was not there. She went to his apartment to make sure he was all right. A young, pretty woman, who was scantily dressed, greeted her at the door. She was petite with blonde hair that reached the middle of her back. Jennie gaped at her.

"May I help you?" asked the girl.

"Is Ran…Randy here?"

"Are you his mother?"

Jennie glared at her. "No, just a friend."

"He can't come to the door right now. He's not dressed," said the girl with a smirk. "What's your name? I'll tell him you're here."

"That's O.K. I'll stop by another time."

Jennie sped down the highway filled with varied emotions: shock, humiliation, used, dirty, to name a few. When she arrived home she was relieved to discover Brenner was not there. After a hot shower, she poured herself a tall glass of straight scotch and glanced into the mirror. The image peering back at her looked very ugly. Jennie gulped down the drink and wondered how many more she would need to feel better.

A couple of hours later Brenner entered the house and found his wife passed out on the couch with an empty bottle of scotch beside her. After covering her with a blanket, he lay alone in bed and realized that he would have to make plans soon to get help for Jennie's drinking problems. His future depended on it.

Chapter Seven

Brenner wrote notes on a clipboard while Jennie tried to concentrate on a historical romance novel.

"Why do I have to go so far away?" asked Jennie.

Brenner stopped writing and frowned. "To ensure that no one finds out about your drinking problem. I'm going to be starting my campaign for president, remember?"

Jennie put her book down and glared at him. "And you want me out of the way."

His lips tightened. "That's not true. You've got a drinking problem. Since you can't stop by yourself, you need help. I want what's best for you."

"You only care about your career, not me."

"Nonsense. I care about you and want you to get well."

Jennie pouted. "I'm not sick."

"We've been through this too many times," said Brenner. "Alcoholism is a disease. It takes lots of help and hard work to recover."

She sat at the edge of her seat and gaped at him. "Are you calling me an alcoholic? That's crazy. I just like an occasional drink to relax."

Brenner put his finger to his lips. "Hush. You're getting loud. Everyone's staring at you."

Jennie put her head back and closed her eyes. "Yeah. They may find out who you are and you'd be in trouble."

"Jennie, please." Brenner let a deep sigh.

"O.K. I'll behave myself."

He patted her hand. "That's my girl."

They did not speak for the rest of the flight. Two hours later they landed in an airport in Nebraska and rented a car. They drove for miles along flat, country roads.

"I can see why it's called "The Cornhusker State," said Jennie. "Look at all the cornfields."

"It's kind of a pretty ride, isn't it?"

"Beautiful. Too bad I couldn't stay at one of those farms. I bet I'd get healthy fast."

Brenner smiled. "Maybe it would be refreshing but you wouldn't have any treatment there."

"Yes I would. I'd be surrounded with clean, fresh air, and open flat land with no traffic and no pollution. I could even do some corn picking." Jennie grinned. "Why don't we move here?"

"That's out of the question. I can't do my job from here."

Jennie glanced at his business suit and laughed. "You would look rather strange in farmer's jeans."

"Very funny," Brenner said. He drove a few miles and took a sharp right. The narrow road led to a group of red brick, two-story buildings. A sign, "Hope Center," was visible in front of the entrance. Jennie trembled while they walked inside the main building.

A nurse in her fifties greeted them. "I'm Mrs. Murphy." She motioned for them to sit down.

"Your names, please?"

"Jennie Sands."

Mrs. Murphy typed the facts into a computer while she questioned them.

"And your name, sir?"

"I assume you're her husband?"

"Yes."

The nurse studied his face. "I've seen you on television. You're Senator Sands. Are you the one being admitted?"

Brenner's face turned deep red. "My wife's the one who's here for help, not me." He leaned forward and spoke softly. "You won't let the press know about this, will you?"

"Definitely not, said Mrs. Murphy with a deep frown. "We don't disclose information about our patients to anyone without their permission. Everything's strictly confidential."

Brenner sighed. "Glad to hear that."

Jennie scowled and shook her head.

After all the data was completed, Mrs. Murphy gave them a tour of the grounds and some facilities, including the dining room and a gigantic spa with various exercise machines, a swimming pool, and a whirlpool.

There was a sparkle in Jennie's eyes when she viewed the pool and hot tub. "I know where I'll be spending most of my time."

"Good," Mrs. Murphy said. "Working out in the spa is highly recommended with your treatment."

They inspected Jennie's room last, which was located in a building near the office.

"I'll leave you two alone now," said the nurse. "If you need me, Mrs. Sands, I'm right next door."

"Thank you, ma'am."

About thirty minutes later, Jennie's suitcases were unpacked and she was settled in her room.

"I've got to leave or I'll miss my plane," said Brenner. He kissed her and held her for a moment.

Tears filled her eyes. "I'm scared. I've never been this far from home before without you."

37

Brenner cradled his wife in his arms and brushed her tears away. "You're going to be just fine. You cooperate with the doctor and you'll be home before you know it."

Jennie hugged her husband. "I'll miss you. When will I see you again?"

"I'll visit you when I can get away. Till then..." Brenner held up her chin and looked into her eyes. "You work on getting well. I know you can do it."

Brenner kissed her and sped out the door.

After he left, Jennie lay on the bed and sobbed. How was she going to make it through this ordeal alone? She closed her eyes and, for the first time in years, prayed.

Brenner was home by late afternoon. He showered and ordered a pizza. In the evening he called all the members of the poker club and arranged for a meeting regarding the campaign after their poker game the following night.

He made one last call. "She's gone..."

About thirty minutes later a hot body slid next to Brenner. They kissed, caressed each other, and made passionate love.

"You feel great, Bunny." Brenner moaned. "It's been so long."

When they were both satisfied they lay still, encircled in each other's arms.

"How long will your wife be gone?" asked Bunny.

"I'm not sure, maybe a month. Wish it could be a lot longer so we could have lots of nights like this."

Bunny nodded, got up, and started to dress.

"Stay with me tonight," said Brenner.

"I'd love to but I can't. You know why."

A few minutes later Brenner was alone in bed. Memories of making love to Bunny lingered while he drifted into a deep sleep.

The following evening everyone was waiting at the club for Brenner. They were just about to start the card game without him when he walked in with another man.

"Guys, I want you to meet my new campaign manager, Rick Allen."

They all greeted him and shook his hand.

"Since we'll all be meeting here every Wednesday after the game to plan the campaign, do you have any objections to Rick playing poker with us?" Brenner asked. "Of course, he'd be an alternate for someone who can't make it."

"No objections," said Peter.

The rest agreed.

Johnny looked at Brenner. "Can we start the game now?"

"Have you noticed the stock market has been dropping lately?" Peter asked as he picked up his cards. "That could be an issue we could use in our campaign."

"To hell with politics." Chuck banged his fist on the table. "Let's save that for our meeting and play cards."

"Right on," Raymond said.

They played poker until eleven o'clock. Then they enjoyed a few drinks and socialized for a few minutes before the meeting started.

"What do you do for a living, Rick?" asked Raymond.

"I'm an attorney."

"Wow!" Johnny raised his drink in the air. "Can I call you when I get in trouble?"

"Anytime."

Chuck placed a drink in front of Brenner. "Hey! I hear you're a bachelor now."

"That's right. Jennie's visiting a friend."

"How long are you going to be free?"

"About a month."

Chuck smiled. "Got any babes lined up?"

"Too busy for that," said Brenner with a red face.

"There's always time for a good woman," chuckled Raymond.

Corey glanced at his watch. "Enough of that talk. Let's start the meeting. It's getting late."

Brenner took out some notes. "He's right. We only have two years until the election and there's so much to do."

"How can we help?" asked Raymond.

"I've made a list of issues and chose each of you to research one." Brenner passed out a copy to everyone. "Ill give you a few minutes to read this, then I'll answer any questions you may have."

About ten minutes later Brenner stood up. "I'm going to read the names I've picked for each issue. If you have any questions or objections, please present them."

"Peter, I put you down for crime. Any comments?"

"Sounds like a big project."

"Crime has escalated in this country, but I believe you handle it. Also you can get others to help."

Peter nodded. "All right. I'll do it."

Brenner peered at Dr. Levin. "I'd like you to be my Surgeon General. Of course, you can't take that position until I'm elected. But you can start the researching of the issues I listed. Do you think you can do this?"

"I'm sure I can," said Dr. Levin with a smile.

"Let me see." Brenner ran his finger down his list. "I need two of you for social issues, since it covers a lot. Johnny and Raymond, can you work of them?"

Johnny nodded. "No problem."

"Piece of cake," Raymond said.

Corey and Chuck were assigned the defense and space programs.

39

"Can't wait to get started," Corey said.

"And you, Chuck?"

He shrugged his shoulders. "Yeah. I'll do it."

Johnny looked at Brenner. "What about you? Anything on the list for you?"

"I'm not getting off easy," Brenner said. "I' taking care of foreign affairs and trade agreements, plus the economy. That should keep me busy." He sipped his drink. "Well, that sums up the issues. I'll meet with you individually in the future to discuss more details. In the meantime, research your assigned issue, find out how it's been handled in the past, and present possible ways to improve it. Any questions?"

"Just one," Chuck said. "How did you find Rick?"

"He's my attorney," Brenner glanced at Rick. "He takes wonderful care of my personal affairs so I know he'll make a great campaign manager."

"I'll do my best," Rick said.

"Anything else?"

"Johnny yawned. "Yeah. Can we go home?"

"Meeting's adjourned," said Brenner.

They all headed for the parking lot. Raymond and Johnny walked together toward their cars and discussed the issues they had to research. They started to cross the street when a big black car appeared out of nowhere, swerved toward the center, then moved directly at them. Raymond yelled and jumped out of the way. Johnny didn't see it in time. The impact of the car tossed him into the air before he bounced off the hook and fell face down on the road. Tires shrieked as the car sped around a curve and raced out of sight.

Everyone dashed to the scene of the accident.

"What happened?" asked Chuck.

"Some maniac hit Johnny and took off," said Raymond.

"Did you get a license plate number?" Brenner asked.

"No. It happened too fast."

Dr. Levin took Johnny's pulse and shook his head. Policemen appeared in minutes and an ambulance soon after. Johnny was pronounced dead at the scene.

Chuck stared at the still, bloody body. "Just what the hell's going on? First Mike, then Bruce, and now Johnny."

Raymond's lower lip quivered while tears filled his eyes. "Unbelievable!"

"This is different," Peter said. "Mike and Bruce died from natural causes. Johnny's death was an accident."

"No way," Raymond said. "That car came right at him. I believe someone hit him intentionally."

"Nonsense. Who would do that?" asked Brenner.

"I don't know," said Raymond. "But maybe that same person wants all of us dead."

Brenner frowned. "Have you any idea who that person could be?"

"All I know is that Johnny told me that he learned something about a couple of members of our group."

"What did he learn and who was he talking about?"

"I don't know. He was too scared to tell me anymore."

"I don't believe you. You two were very close." Brenner scowled at Raymond. "He must have confided in you. You have to tell me so we can get to the bottom of this."

Raymond's body trembled while he shook his head. "Damn it. I don't know anything more than what I told you. Drop it, will you?"

Brenner patted his back lightly. "O.K…O.K. You don't have to get so upset."

Chuck yelled. "Knock it off, both of you."

Corey intervened. "Our imaginations are going wild. I think we all need some sleep. It's been a long day."

"Right," said Peter. "It doesn't help to get nervous with each other. Let's get out of here."

They all left feeling exhausted but knew they would not sleep well that night.

On the way home, Raymond's words about Johnny kept repeating in Brenner's mind.

Did Johnny reveal to Raymond what he had discovered about a couple of members of the club? And what members was he referring to?

It was important to find out if Johnny disclosed those names to Raymond, or anyone else.

Chapter Eight

The doorbell rang about eight in the morning. Brenner's housekeeper, Martha, scampered to the door. A tall, slim man in his thirties showed her a badge. "I'm Detective Joe Griffin. Is Brenner Sands at home?"

"Yes. He's eating breakfast."

"Could I talk to him, please? It's important."

"Come with me, sir."

Martha led him into the dining room. "Mr. Sands, sorry to interrupt your breakfast, but Detective Griffin is here to see you. He said it's important."

Brenner stood up and shook his hand. "What can I do for you?"

"I need to ask you a few questions."

Brenner sipped his coffee. "Martha, bring Detective Griffin a cup of coffee, please."

A few minutes later she served him the coffee and stared at Brenner with her hands clasped across her thick belly.

"That'll be all. You may go now."

Martha left the room and continued her chores.

Brenner looked at the detective. "Now, what kind of questions do you have for me?"

"I'm investigating the death of Johnny Ruben. What do you know about him?"

"He was a senator, and a very good one."

"Were you friends?"

"Yes. We played poker together."

"Who else played with you?"

Brenner told him their names while the detective scribbled them down on a small pad.

When he finished writing he looked up at Brenner. "When was the last time you saw Johnny?"

"Wednesday."

"What were you doing?"

"Playing cards."

The detective stared at him. "That was the night Johnny was killed, right?"

"Yes, but his death was an accident. Why all the questions?"

"It was a hit and run. I'm looking for information that may lead to the one who hit him."

"I can't help you there," Brenner said.

"Did you see Johnny get hit?" asked the detective.

"No. I was walking the other way."

"What about after he was hit?"

Brenner's lower lip quivered. "I saw him lying in the road in a pool of blood."

"Did you see the car that hit him?"

"I caught a glimpse of the back of it as it sped a way. I think it was black, I'm not sure."

"What type of car was it?"

"Don't know."

Detective Griffin ran his fingers through his black, wavy hair. "Isn't this the third member of congress to die within two months?"

"Yes."

"Did the other two belong to your poker club?"

"Yes." Brenner frowned. "What are you implying?"

The detective tapped his pen on the table. "Nothing. These are just routine questions. What did they die from?"

"Natural causes."

Detective Griffin smiled and stood up. "That's all I have for now. Thanks. You've been very helpful."

Brenner walked him to the door. "Call me if you hear anything."

"I will. Also, I'll be talking to the other members of the club soon. Maybe one of them saw something."

"I hope you find the bastard who killed Johnny," said Brenner.

"I'll do my best." Detective Griffin shook his hand and walked out the door.

Brenner went back to the dining room and pondered on the detective's visit over another cup of hot coffee. The phone rang and he jumped up to answer it.

"Jennie. It's good to hear your voice. How are you doing?"

"A lot better. When are you going to visit me?"

"As soon as I can get away." Brenner hesitated. "I've got to go to another funeral."

"What are you talking about? Who died?"

"Johnny Ruben."

"Oh, my God! Johnny died? How did it happen?"

"He was hit by a car."

"Was it a DUI?"

Brenner sighed. "They don't know. It was a hit and run. A detective was just here asking questions."

"Why? Does he think you had something to do with it?"

"No. He didn't accuse me of anything. He said it was just routine, but he sure did ask a lot of questions."

"It all sounds scary to me. You'd better be careful."

"I'm fine. Don't worry. This is all a coincidence."

"Hope you're right. So, when can you visit? I miss you."

"I'll be there after the funeral, in a few days."

43

"I'll see you then. I love you," said Jennie.

"Me, too."

There was a large gathering for the funeral services of Johnny. All the senators were present along with most of the other members of congress. He didn't have a wife or children, but some of his family that did attend included his parents and five brothers and sisters.

Raymond Masters said the eulogy. "Johnny was a very dear friend who was always there when we needed him. I'm going to miss him." His voice cracked. "We're all going to miss him."

He wiped the tears from his face.

When the services were completed, the members of the poker club carried the casket to the hearse. Rain fell softly on the roof of the vehicle while it crept off in the direction of the cemetery.

The Aces High poker players met at the club after the funeral. They ordered drinks and toasted Johnny.

Chuck raised his glass. "This is for you, guy. You were one of the best. I'm going to miss you."

Raymond pointed to a chair. "That's your chair, buddy. It's not right, just not right." He hung his head and cried.

After the rest of the members toasted Johnny, they sat in silence for a while.

"Any more deaths and we'll be alcoholics," said Chuck.

Everyone forced a smile.

"Did a Detective Griffin visit any of you about Johnny's death?" asked Brenner.

"He came to my house," said Corey.

"Did he ask a lot of questions?" asked Brenner.

"Yeah, a lot about what I witnessed at the accident," Corey said. "He's looking for the person who hit Johnny."

Brenner learned that the detective had contacted all the members of the club and had asked them basically the same questions.

"He also inquired about Bruce and Mike and how they died," Raymond said. "Why would he ask about them?"

Chuck's face turned crimson. "Maybe he thinks they were murdered, Johnny too."

Peter shook his head. "That's absurd. We all know how they died. Chuck, don't let your imagination run away with you."

"Do we really know how they died?" asked Chuck.

"I gave you the results of the autopsies," said Dr. Levin. "Are you doubting my diagnoses?"

"No. I guess I'm just exhausted from all this," Chuck said. "Sorry."

Brenner stood up. "It's been a long day. Let's go home and get some rest."

Everyone agreed and left.

Later that evening Brenner made a phone call. "Can you get away?"

In a short while Brenner's heart raced fiercely as he hugged his lover. "Bunny, oh Bunny. I need you so badly. Help me release the tensions that are smoldering inside me."

They made love until their passions were realized, then fell asleep in each other's arms.

Brenner woke up alone about seven-thirty in the morning. Memories of Bunny remained in his mind and made him feel warm all over.

The phone rang. "Are you coming today?"

A twinge of guilt engulfed him. "I was just about to leave."

Brenner laid his head back on the head rest part of the seat and closed his eyes while the plane traveled across country. He rehearsed in his mind what he would say to Jennie. He had to be gentle, understanding, and affectionate. It was important to get Jennie well so she could work with him on the campaign.

He arrived at Hope Center several hours later and walked up to the front desk.

Mrs. Murphy peered over her glasses that rested on her round face and smiled at him. "Mr. Sands. How may I help you?"

"May I please see my wife?"

She picked up the phone. "I'll see if she's in her room."

A couple of minutes later she said, "She's waiting for you. You'll be happy to see how well she's doing."

"Is her doctor here?" asked Brenner. "I'd like to see him before I leave."

Mrs. Murphy made another call. "He's here today. He said he can see you in an hour."

Brenner smiled. "You do good work."

She giggled. "Oh, thank you Mr. Sands."

He approached his wife's room, took a deep breath, and knocked on the door. Jennie greeted him with a glowing face and sparkling eyes.

She put her arms around his neck. "I'm so happy to see you."

He gave her a quick kiss then held her at arm's length. "You look beautiful, just wonderful. And your hair looks great. It seems longer."

"I decided to let it grow."

"I like it. Do you feel as good as you look?'

"I feel great. Now can I go home?"

"We've got to see your doctor in a little while," said Brenner. "He'll tell us when you can go home."

With their hands clasped, they chatted all the way to the doctor's office. Brenner and Jennie sat directly across from Dr. Aldrich.

The doctor shook Brenner's hand. "Glad you could make it."

"How's Jennie doing?" asked Brenner.

"Just fine. She's been cooperating well."

Jennie grinned. "Then I can go home with my husband?"

Dr. Aldrich shook his head. "Sorry. Not this time."

"Why not?"

"You're not ready. I recommend that you attend more group therapy meetings."

"How long will that take?"

"You should be ready to go home in two weeks, if you don't have any setbacks."

She frowned. "I'm ready now."

Brenner put his arm around her shoulder. "If you go home too soon, you may have to return for more treatment. Two more weeks isn't that long."

"Easy for you to say," Jennie said.

"Your husband's right," said Dr. Aldrich. "If you go home too early and return here, you would have to start the program over and may have to stay twice as long."

Jennie pouted. "Looks like I don't have much of a choice. All right. I'll stay two more weeks, but no longer."

"Good girl," said Brenner.

Dr. Aldrich looked at him. "Mr. Sands, do you know anything about your wife's problem?"

"All I know is once she starts drinking she can't stop."

"Why does she drink?"

"I don't know. She says she drinks to relax."

"Jennie is a lonely woman because you're gone so much," said the doctor. "If she had more to do, she may be able to fight her problem better."

Brenner smiled. "She's going to have plenty to do when she gets back. She'll be helping me with my campaign."

"Campaign?"

"Yes, my campaign for president."

Dr. Aldrich raised his eyebrows. "I didn't realize you were running for president.

I agree. That should help keep Jennie busy."

"Anything else I need to know?" asked Brenner.

"There is one more thing. Jennie seems to lack sufficient sex. She says that you reject her often, leaving her frustrated. If you have a problem, perhaps a doctor can help you."

Brenner glanced at Jennie while she lowered her eyes. "I don't need a doctor. I work very hard and am too tired for sex most of the time."

"I know it's difficult with your schedule, but try to cut down on your work, at least weekends. Perhaps you could take your wife out once a week, relax, and let sex happen naturally."

Brenner sighed. "I'll work on it."

"That's all we can expect from you," said Dr. Aldrich. He turned to Jennie. "You've got to work hard at this too. There must be support groups in your area that you can go to and call on when you get the urge for a drink."

"I'm sure there are. I'll check into it when I get back," Jennie said. "I probably won't have time to go often because I'll be so busy with the campaign."

"But you must contact someone if necessary," the doctor said. "It's essential to your recovery."

"Good. Any other questions?" asked Dr. Aldrich.

"Do I have your permission to take my wife off grounds for a few hours?"

The doctor looked at his watch. "Yes. It would do her good. Let's see. It's two o'clock now. Can you have her back by five?"

"I sure can."

They got up, shook the doctor's hand, and left.

Jennie grinned when they walked toward the car. "Thanks, Brenner. It'll be great to get away from here for a while."

They drove along the countryside on their way to town.

"Those cornfields seem to extend forever," Brenner said.

"Yes, and look at those huge cattle farms," said Jennie. "I love this area. Could we move here, please?"

"Perhaps after we retire."

"I don't want to wait that long."

Brenner pondered for a moment. "We could buy a piece of land for our retirement."

"Today?"

"Not today. I have to catch my plane at seven," Brenner said. "We'll talk about it when I come back to get you in two weeks."

Jennie snuggled closer to her husband. "That sounds terrific."

After a few miles of driving in silence, Brenner glanced at his wife. "By the way, I didn't appreciate the way you discussed our love life with Dr. Aldrich. Do you think that was necessary?"

"He asked me about it. Did you want me to lie?"

Brenner shook his head. "You just didn't have to say anything."

"What bothered you the most about what I told him?"

"You didn't have to tell him that I rejected you."

"It's the truth."

Brenner frowned. "You always approached me when I was tired."

"Most of the time you rejected me no matter when I approached you."

"You're exaggerating," said Brenner. "Anyway, what's sex got to do with your drinking problem?"

"Dr. Aldrich said that if I were more content with my sex life, my craving for a drink could diminish."

"That's ridiculous. I don't believe that."

47

They arrived in town about thirty minutes later. Jennie pointed to a motel. "Why don't we stop there? Let us see if Dr. Aldrich is right."

"Come on, Jennie. You've got to be back by five."

"You're rejecting me again."

"That's not true. We would be too rushed. I fear that I would fail and you would get upset." Brenner took a deep breath. "Let's wait until we have more time and let it happen naturally, like your doctor suggested."

"I didn't know you feared not being able to perform in bed. Why didn't you tell me?"

"How do you tell your wife you are scared to have sex with her because you might not be able to do it?"

"You just did. Now that I know how you feel, I'll try to be more patient from now on."

"I'm not so sure you can be more tolerant," said Brenner. "But I do feel I need to get some help with performing better in bed."

"If you think you need help, check into it."

He pulled up in front of a restaurant. "Hungry?"

"Starved."

They entered the restaurant and were seated near a window. Tablecloths with white geese and a blue background covered the tables. Pictures of farm scenes and cornfields hung on the walls. The waitress wore blue dresses with white aprons and white bonnets.

"What a cheerful place," Jennie said.

"I feel like I'm in the country."

Jennie giggled. "You are. Isn't it great?"

Brenner shrugged his shoulders. "A pleasant contrast to the city."

Jennie peered out the window and saw some people going in and out of stores.

"It's good to see some normal people," she said.

"Normal?"

"The ones in the hospital are nice, but they always talk about their problems. These people look happy, more normal."

Brenner laughed. "If you say so."

A waitress smiled at them. "May I take your order?"

"I want spaghetti and meat balls and a salad, please."

Brenner stared at her. "You can have more than that."

Jennie shook her head. "I'm in the mood for spaghetti."

"All right," said Brenner. "I'll have steak, well done, a baked potato, and corn on the cob."

"Oh, I'll have a side dish of corn on the cob," Jennie said. "I've got to try the corn here."

"You won't be sorry," said the waitress.

In a short while the hot food was placed in front of them.

"The spaghetti's great," Jennie said. "And this corn is fabulous. Have you ever tasted anything like it?"

Brenner rubbed his tummy. "No, I haven't. This is a wonderful dinner. We'll have to stop here again."

"Definitely," said Jennie as she stood up." Now can we walk for a while? I want some exercise after all that wonderful food."

"Sure," said Brenner. "Let's look at some of the stores."

Jennie grinned. "Great. I haven't shopped in a long time."

After going in and out of most of the stores, Jennie found a mint-green dress with matching shoes that she liked. She looked at her husband. "Should I get them?"

"Yes. You look pretty in that color."

Jennie blushed. "Thanks. See anything you want?"

"Nothing." Brenner glanced at his watch. "Hate to spoil your fun, but you've got to get back. We'll just about make it if we leave now."

As they drove toward Hope Center, Jennie said, "This is the best day I've had in a long time. Wish it didn't have to end."

"They'll be more," Brenner said. "You get well and we'll have many days like this, even better."

When Brenner brought Jennie back to her room, she clung to him. "I'm going to miss you."

He brushed her auburn hair away from her face. "You'll be just fine. Remember, two more weeks and you'll be home."

Brenner kissed Jennie and hurried out the door.

He got aboard the plane just as it was about to take off. He found his seat, took a few deep breaths, put his head back, and closed his eyes.

He needed Jennie to help him win the election. It would require hard work to keep her happy.

Could he fulfill his promise to her, to let sex happen naturally in the future?

Brenner felt pangs around his heart when he realized what he must do soon. He would have to stop seeing his lover, Bunny, for a while.

That would be the greatest sacrifice of all.

Chapter Nine

Brenner got out of the shower, dried his dripping body, and laid on the bed, eagerly waiting for his lover. He dozed for a few moments, then woke up to Bunny's tongue traveling over every part of his body. Tingling sensations ran up and down his spine. Their hot bodies met and exploded with passion until they both felt fulfilled.

Brenner held Bunny. "This is ecstasy, pure ecstasy."

Bunny smiled, slipped away, and got dressed.

"We'll have to see each other as much as possible before Jennie comes home."

"When I can get away." Bunny kissed him and went out the door.

The next night everyone met to play poker. After the game, they held a campaign meeting to discuss the progress of the programs.

"Peter, did you do any research on crime?" asked Brenner.

"Yes. Violent crime is rising at a rapid pace, especially among juveniles. We've got to find out why this is happening and what can be done to stop or reduce these crimes committed by the young hoodlums and others."

"Sounds like you have a real challenge, Peter. But I've got confidence in you that you will come up with some good solutions to handling these situations."

He turned to Raymond. "Do you have anything?"

Raymond nodded. "Most of all, people worry about their social security. They feel the government has misused this money and they want it stopped."

"Any truth to this?" asked Brenner.

"Of course." Raymond scowled. "You've been working long enough for the government to know it's true. Our job is to convince the people that we're the only ones who will protect their money."

"Promise them anything," Brenner said. "As long as you get their votes, that is all that matters."

Suddenly the door to the meeting room opened and Detective Griffin approached them. "Sorry to interrupt you, but I must talk with you."

"What's wrong now?" asked Chuck.

"Actually I've got good news. The guy who hit Johnny Ruben was arrested."

"How did you find him?" asked Brenner.

"He was stopped for speeding in a nearby town. The officer discovered the vehicle was stolen and arrested him."

Raymond clenched his fists. "What's the bum's name?"

"Hugo Scully, who is a repeat offender."

Tears filled Raymond's eyes. "I hope you hang the bastard."

"How did you know he was the one who hit him?" Brenner asked.

"Blood on the bumper of the car matched Johnny's blood."

Chuck's face was crimson. "Where's the derelict now?"

"In jail, until he goes to court."

"Court? That's a joke," Corey said. "They will slap his wrist and set him free. Then he will kill someone else."

Detective Griffin shook his head. "Not with the charges pending against him. Stealing a car, leaving the scene of an accident, and vehicular homicide, to name a few. He has other outstanding warrants too. That should put him away for a long time."

"I certainly hope so," said Brenner.

"I'll be in touch if I hear any news," said the detective as he walked out the door.

Raymond pounded the table. "Damn...damn. Why Johnny?" His voice escalated. "Why couldn't have been me?"

"Maybe it was meant to be Johnny," Chuck said.

"What do you mean?" asked Raymond.

Chuck shrugged shoulders. "I don't know. I think there's something fishy going on."

"Are you saying that someone wanted Johnny dead?"

"Maybe."

Brenner stood up and held up some folders. "You're both talking crazy. Let's calm down and finish our reports."

"Sorry, I'm too upset to stay," said Raymond while he dashed out the door.

"Hope he's going to be all right," Chuck said.

"Me, too," said Peter. "He's got to stop blaming himself for the accident. There was nothing he could have done."

Brenner shook his head. "Are we going to talk about this all night? Let's get going with our meeting."

"Count me out," Chuck said and grabbed his coat.

The rest stood up and started to leave.

"We only have two reports to do," Brenner said.

"Looks like no one is interested," said Corey.

Brenner sighed. "Guess we will have to wait to next week to finish. Meeting is adjourned."

He rushed home and climbed into bed. With a thumping heart, he slipped into Bunny's waiting arms.

"Make me feel good," said Brenner.

They kissed long and hard then made love until their bodies went limp.

"I love you so much, Bunny. I wish this could last forever."

"Me, too."

Brenner took a deep breath. "Looks like forever is almost here. Jennie is coming home."

"Damn. We won't be able to see each other as much."

"In fact, not at all."

Bunny jumped up. "What are you talking about?"

"I can't take any chances now," Brenner said. "I can't risk Jennie finding out about us, especially with the campaign about to start. I need her by my side, with us portraying a loving couple to the public."

"And I have just been a toy to you," Bunny said.

"No way," said Brenner. "Jennie means nothing to me. It's just a big show for votes."

Brenner embraced Bunny. "You are my true love. I wish you could be by my side, not Jennie. But you know it is impossible."

Bunny broke away from Brenner, climbed out of bed and got dressed. "I'd better go now."

"Wait. Stay a few minutes longer, please."

"The longer I wait, the harder it is." Bunny rushed out the door.

Brenner tossed and turned for hours. The love making scenes that he cherished replayed continuously in his mind, ending with the same question...

How could he live without Bunny?"

Another challenge would have to be faced when Jennie got home, making love to her.

Would he fail again?

Chapter Ten

The flight to Nebraska seemed like an eternity. Brenner attempted to read a book but found it hard to concentrate. He read the same paragraph over and over until the words blurred. In frustration, he slammed the book down.

The man in the seat next to him looked at him out of the corner of this eye. "I'm Rob. What's your name?"

"Brenner."

"You look like something's bothering you," said Rob. "Want to talk about it?"

Brenner's face was crimson. "Nothing's wrong."

"Then why did you throw your book down so hard? It scared me."

"It slipped out of my hand."

"Nevertheless, if you need to talk to someone about anything, you can discuss it with me," Rob said. "I'm a good listener."

"Thanks for your concern but I've been working a lot lately and I'm exhausted. There's nothing more to it."

Brenner leaned his head back and closed his eyes. Rob put on his headphones and tapped his fingers on the armrest in rhythm to the music playing in his ears.

Brenner's mind raced from picking up Jennie at Hope Center to their first night alone in their bed. He reached for a soda with trembling hands and took deep breaths to try to calm down.

"Are you sure you're O.K.?" Rob asked.

"I'm fine, thank you."

Brenner put on his headphones, listened to classical music, and started to calm down. He was almost asleep when he felt a jolt. The plane moved up and dropped down in quick intervals. People near him gasped.

The pilot spoke over the intercom. "Don't be alarmed. We are passing through a thunderstorm. This turbulence should only last a few minutes. For your safety, fasten your seat belts."

Rain pounded against the windows and lightning flashed around the plane. Brenner's heart raced. He wondered if the plane was going to crash.

Rob peered at the storm. "Looks pretty scary out there."

"It'll pass," said Brenner. "We'll make it...don't worry."

"Hope you're right." Rob's hands shook. "I try not to show it, but I dread flying."

"Why don't you travel another way?"

"My job takes me all over the country. The fastest way I can get there is by plane."

"That's a dilemma," said Brenner. "Ever take that course given by the airlines to help you get over your fear of flying?"

"Twice. It didn't help."

"Maybe you ought to change jobs."

Rob nodded. "I'm seriously thinking of it, if we make it through this."

"We will."

The plane rocked back and forth. Rob bit his bottom lip and clenched his fists. "Oh, God. We're going to crash."

"Think of beautiful things," said Brenner. "Do you have a wife?"

"Yes, a gorgeous wife. I should be with her right now."

"Put your headphones on and turn on some soft music. Imagine that you are holding your wife close while you dance."

Rob's hands trembled and his breathing increased rapidly while he put on the headphones. In short a while his breathing slowed down and a smile appeared on his face.

Brenner sighed and looked out the window. He observed that the rain had subsided and the plane moved smoothly again.

Rob looked out the window and grinned. "Look! "You were right. We passed through the storm with no problems."

"Of course."

"Weren't you a little scared?"

Brenner shrugged his shoulders. "A little."

"When I get back, I'm going to look for another job close to home so I won't have to fly," Rob said.

"Good idea."

"My wife will be happy too. She hates being alone so much. Do you have a wife, Brenner?"

"Yes."

"I bet you're anxious to see her, too."

"Yeah, anxious."

A couple of hours later the plane landed in Nebraska.

Rob shook Brenner's hand. "Thanks for being a good listener. And you helped me a lot getting through that scary ordeal."

"No problem."

Brenner got off the plane and rented a car. He drove slowly along the countryside and rehearsed what he would say to Jennie, at times repeating the words out loud. Shortly afterwards he parked in front of Hope Center. His hands quivered when he opened the car door and ascended the steps to the administration office.

Jennie was seated near Mrs. Murphy. When she saw Brenner, she ran to him and threw her arms around him.

"I'm so happy to see you, so very happy." She kissed him and squeezed him hard.

Brenner broke away from Jennie and stared at her. "You look wonderful, Jennie. Do you feel as good as you look?"

"I feel terrific. I'm cured."

"Is she ready to go, Mrs. Murphy?"

"You've got to fill out some papers, see the doctor, and after that, you may take your wife home."

It took about ten minutes for Brenner to take care of the paper work.

Jennie hugged Mrs. Murphy. "Thanks for all you did for me. You were terrific."

"It was easy working with you," said the nurse. "Take good care of yourself."

They both proceeded to meet with her doctor.

"Jennie is doing very well," Dr. Aldrich said. "If she stays away from the liquor when she gets home, she will do fine."

"You will be good, won't you?" asked Brenner.

Jennie smiled. "I'll make you proud of me."

"AA meetings should help," Dr. Aldrich said.

"I'll check on them when I get home," Brenner said.

"Good. Her chances of staying well are better if she can talk to people with similar problems."

Brenner glanced at Jennie. "I've also made arrangements with our housekeeper, Martha, to stay with us for a while, to keep a close eye on Jennie. She will make sure she doesn't drink."

Jennie winced.

"I like that idea," the doctor said. "She won't be alone and tempted to drink. Between having someone with her in the daytime and meetings at night, Jennie should be fine."

"I am sure of it," Brenner said.

"You're both talking like I am not here," Jennie said. "Are you two intentionally leaving me out of your conversation?"

"No way," said her doctor. "Brenner and I are discussing the best ways for your care. Sorry if you felt left out."

"I regret that you misunderstood us," Brenner said. "It was not intentional."

"All right. I believe you." Jennie stood up. "Are we finished discussing my problems? I'm ready to go home."

"If you two have no more questions, you're free to go," said Dr. Aldrich.

Jennie hugged Dr. Aldrich. "Thank you for everything. I appreciate all you've done for me."

"You were a good patient."

Brenner picked up her suitcases and they walked out the door.

Jennie paused on the steps and took a long, deep breath. "That fresh air smells wonderful."

"Let's get going. We don't want to miss our flight," Brenner said.

Jennie scurried to the car, got in, and snuggled close to her husband. "No, I don't want to miss the plane. I've been waiting too long to go home. I'm anxious to get there, Brenner. It's been so hard being without you and our home."

"I only hope you keep your word and stay sober."

Jennie shrugged. "Don't worry. That will be easy."

"Nothing is easy, Jennie. You will have to work at it."

She leaned her head back while they rode in silence.

Jennie spoke first. "Does Martha now about my stay at the center?"

"Yes."

"I can't believe it. You told her I'm a drunk?"

"Not exactly. I said you've got a problem with drinking."

"What problem?" I just like an occasional drink."

"Sure. All you need to take is one drink and you can't stop." He shook his finger at her. "No more booze for you…ever."

Jennie sighed. "Then why do I need Martha to watch me if I won't be drinking?"

"To make sure you don't start again."

Her eyes were downcast. "That will make me feel like I am in prison with Martha, my jailer."

"Nonsense. She'll be your companion, not your jailer. You won't feel so lonely when I'm working long hours."

"Was she your companion while I was gone?"

"No," said Brenner. "She took care of the chores and left."

Jennie pouted. "I guess you didn't have to be watched."

"Stop being so difficult."

She crossed her arms in front of her. "What about the AA meetings? Are you going to make me go to those, too?"

"No. I can't take a chance of the media finding out and possibly using it against me during my campaign for president."

Jennie let out deep sigh. "Thank God. Even though your reasoning is selfish, as usual, nevertheless, I don't want to go among all those drunks."

He patted her hand. "Figured you would agree. But I don't think my thinking is selfish, just realistic."

"Whatever…"

Brenner pointed to the cornfields. "Take a last look at them. What a beautiful sight."

Jennie sat up and viewed at the countryside. "I hope it's not the last time we see these farms. You promised to buy some land here, remember?"

"I said possibly for our retirement. We've got a long way to go."

"Maybe we can take a vacation here soon."

"Slow down, Jennie. Don't forget, we've got a lot of work to do for the campaign."

She sighed. "You're right. When do I start helping?"

"You can get together with the other wives shortly after we get back."

"What do I say to them about where I've been?"

Brenner's lips were firm when he spoke. "You were visiting a friend. That's what I told the guys. You must never, never tell them your problem and where you've been. If the truth got out to the press, it would ruin my chances for becoming president."

"You're just worried about your image, not me."

"I care about us," Brenner said. "You do want to be First Lady, don't you?"

Jennie shrugged. "I guess so."

"That's why we've got to be careful about people finding out about your drinking problem."

"I can see the headlines now," laughed Jennie. "The future First Lady is a drunk."

"Stop it, Jennie. That's not funny."

She tapped his arm lightly. "Loosen up. I was only joking."

"I don't appreciate those kind of jokes."

"Sorry. I can't be up tight like you all the time. I love to have fun."

"Certain things aren't funny. You've got to learn the difference, especially when we are campaigning."

Jennie snickered. "Perhaps I should go to charm school."

"Perhaps."

Jennie laid her head back and pretended to sleep all the way to the airport.

When they boarded the plane, Jennie sat next to the window. "I can't believe it. I'm on my way home. Isn't it wonderful?"

Brenner smiled. "It's terrific."

After they were in the air, a stewardess approached them. "Would you like drinks?"

"Oh, Brenner just one glass of champagne to celebrate my coming home, please."

Brenner looked at the stewardess. "Just two cokes, ma'am."

When she left, Brenner glared at Jennie while he spoke in low tones. "For God's sake, Jennie, we're not home yet and you want to break your promise about drinking."

"It's because I'm so happy."

"You can't drink anymore, understand?" He frowned. "Whether you're happy, sad, nervous...whatever. Read my lips. No more drinking."

"All right. You win, as usual."

"You will be the winner if you stay sober, remember that."

"Right," Jennie said. "But it won't be easy. Whenever I feel frustrated or unhappy, I reach for a drink. Guess I'll have to find other ways to unwind."

"Maybe you can go back to the spa for the exercise programs and swimming. That may help."

"Will I have to take Martha with me?"

"Yes."

"Oh, brother."

"I'm sure she'll enjoy going with you."

"Yeah. I bet. The entire idea is ridiculous."

"But necessary."

Jennie pouted. "Staying at Hope center seems easier."

Brenner shook his head. "Can you please be more cooperative about this?"

"I am trying but I do not feel that I require a personal security guard."

"Damn it. Companion."

"A companion does not spy on you."

"You are impossible. Martha is staying with you full time and that's final." Brenner took a deep breath and exhaled.

Jennie wiggled close to her husband. "I know what would calm me down and help me be nice to Martha."

"I'm afraid to ask. What?"

"You make love to me every night and I'll be so content that I will be absolutely no trouble. I guarantee it."

"Figured you'd say something like that."

"Sounds great to me. What about you?"

"I think you're oversexed. That's all you seem to think about," said Brenner with a scowl. "I work long hours and get very tired. No way can I perform every night."

"You can't seem to perform any time. I am not oversexed. I think about it a lot because I don't get enough sex."

Brenner's face turned red. "I do want to satisfy you more often. Perhaps we can get away for a weekend once in a while, like Dr. Aldrich advised. Possibly we will have some success if we let it happen naturally."

Jennie smirked. "Are we going to bring Martha along to watch and offer suggestions?"

"No!"

People turned around and looked at them.

"Everyone is staring at us," Brenner said. "You are getting me too excited."

"Great. It's about time I got you aroused."

Brenner glared at her. "I should have left you at Hope Center." He put his headphones on, turned on relaxing music, and closed his eyes. Jennie began reading a love story with some explicit love scenes. She imagined Brenner as her lover.

After a few hours, Jennie peeked out the window. "Looks like we are getting ready to land."

Brenner took off his headphones and leaned toward the window. "You're right. The plane is descending."

"I can't wait to get home."

"It won't be long."

The plane landed in a short while. They got their luggage and took a cab home.

As they walked toward the front door, Jennie stopped suddenly and put her hands on her hips. "I don't see any bars on the windows. Didn't you have time to put them on?"

Brenner scowled. "You never stop, do you?"

"Sorry." She looked downward. "I was only kidding."

"Once again, you are not funny."

"Guess I'm going to have to work on that."

Martha greeted them at the door. "Welcome home, Mr. and Mrs. Sands. How was your flight?"

"Not bad," said Brenner.

Once inside Brenner looked at Martha. "Doesn't Jennie look great?"

"Oh, yes. You look wonderful. Hope you're feeling better, ma'am."

Jennie forced a smile. "I'm fine."

"Martha, I'm giving you the night off," Brenner said. "I want to be alone with my wife tonight."

Martha's eyes sparkled while she nodded. "I understand, sir. Can't blame you for wanting her to yourself. She's such a pretty lady."

Jennie blushed. "Why thank you, Martha."

As Martha was leaving, she hesitated. "Sir, your dinner is in the oven. You should eat it soon while it is still warm."

"Thanks, Martha. You think of everything," Brenner said. "Enjoy your night off."

"I will. And you two enjoy each other." She giggled and dashed out the door.

"Martha is rather sweet," Jennie said. "I've always liked her. Your plan may work out."

"I'm sure it will. Now let's see what she cooked for us. I am starved."

The table was set with Jennie's favorite crystal and china, with candles in front of each setting. Brenner opened the oven and took out a scrumptious looking roast beef, with browned potatoes, carrots, gravy, and homemade biscuits. He put the food on the table and lit the candles.

"Wow! This looks great," said Jennie. "I'm getting to like Martha more each minute."

"She's a terrific cook, as you know. Dig in."

They were almost finished when the doorbell rang.

"Why don't you get it, Jennie? I'm too full to move."

When she opened the door a man stared back at her. "Are you Jennie Sands?"

"Yes. What can I do for you?"

"These are for you." He handed her a bouquet of long-stemmed red roses. Jennie covered her mouth and gasped. "Thank you."

Jennie walked back to the dining room with the roses. She pulled out a card and read the following words: 'For the only woman in my life. Welcome home. Love, Brenner.'

"Oh, Brenner. What a wonderful surprise," she said with misty eyes. "The roses are absolutely beautiful. Thank you."

She gave him a big kiss.

"It's great to have you home, sweetheart," said Brenner.

Jennie put the roses in a vase with water and placed them in the center of the table. "Let's relax in the den."

Brenner followed her to the couch. Jennie snuggled beside her husband and put her head on his shoulder.

"This has been a wonderful day, thanks to you."

"I just want to make you happy."

Jennie turned on soft music and grabbed his hand. "You can make me happy by dancing with me. It's been so long."

While they danced with a slow rhythm, Jennie pressed hard against his body. She envisioned Brenner picking her up in his arms and dashing into the bedroom, like in the movie, "Gone With The Wind." Her heart raced.

Jennie broke away from him. "Why don't you sit a few minutes while I get comfortable?"

A short while later she appeared in a black, slinky negligee, slit from her waist to the floor.

Brenner whistled. "You're pretty sexy, lady."

She coaxed him to dance again. While moving her satiny gown against his body, she felt a bulge in his pants. Jennie took his hand and led him into the bedroom.

In minutes they lay naked, encircled in each other's arms.

Jennie said, "Make me happy, baby. Make love to me. I want you so bad."

Once again Brenner tried but failed to perform.

"What's the matter? You seemed aroused."

"I don't know. Something's wrong. Maybe it's physical, or maybe it's mental. I just don't know. I'll have to see Dr. Levin for help."

"Don't worry. We will work out. Until then, I'll do my best to have patience with you."

Brenner kissed her forehead. "Thanks."

He lay awake for hours wondering if he would ever be able to satisfy his wife.

Chapter Eleven

Brenner arranged a special meeting on Monday evening to discuss the campaign.

"The time has come to declare my candidacy for president," Brenner said. "Rick, could you set up a news conference for the announcement, hopefully next week?"

"I'll get on it first thing in the morning."

"Great."

"What can we do to help?" Corey asked.

"Organize your notes and what you've researched so far, in case I need information about the issues."

"I've got some new facts since we last met."

"Terrific," Brenner said. "I'd like an update on all the topics. We will start with you, Corey."

"I did some research on the military and discovered it's been cut way back. We have to start building up our armed forces and missile system so we will not be vulnerable to an attack."

Brenner nodded. "This is critical to the safety of our country."

Next, Dr. Levin presented some ideas to cut costs on health care for a more efficient system.

"Good work," said Brenner. "Rising health costs are a main concern of the people."

"Anyone else have anything to add?"

Raymond responded. "As far as taxes go, if we reduce government spending, we will be able to cut taxes, and give money back to the people."

"That idea should hook lots of votes."

Brenner pulled out a stack of papers. "I've done some researching too, about trade agreements." He passed out copies to everyone. "Since it's too long to read now, you can read it during your spare time and offer any suggestions you may have when we meet again."

He gazed at the group. "Does anyone else have new information to share with us?"

They all shook their heads.

"You all have been working very hard. Keep up the good work." Rick said.

"One more thing," said Brenner. "Could I have two copies of your reports that you have completed so far, one for me and one for Rick?"

Raymond frowned. "Mine is not very neat."

"No problem. As long as I have something to refer to for the news conference."

They all agreed to make copies and get them to Brenner.

After one drink and some light conversation, they headed home.

Brenner stopped Dr. Levin on the way out. "I've got to see you as soon as possible. It's rather important."

"What's your problem?"

"I'm having trouble with my sex life and could use some help."

Dr. Levin smiled. "Stop by tomorrow at one o'clock and I will check you and see what I can do for you."

Brenner sighed. "Thanks. I hope you can help me."

The next afternoon Dr. Levin examined him. "I can't find anything seriously wrong with you. What is the major problem when you have sex?"

"When Jennie and I try to make love I can't get an erection. It's important that I satisfy her and I can't."

"Hold on a minute." The doctor went in the next room. He handed Brenner a container full of pills. "Try these. Take one pill an hour before you have sex. It should give you a good erection. Give me a call in a couple of days and tell me if they worked."

"Great! I hope they work and I can please Jennie."

Later that evening Brenner and Jennie were sitting on the couch watching television.

Jennie gazed at her husband. "Have you seen Dr. Levin yet?"

"I saw him today."

"What did he recommend?"

"He gave me pills to take one hour before sex."

Her voice escalated. "Did you take one?"

"Yes." He hesitated. "An hour ago."

Jennie jumped up and grabbed his hand. "What are we waiting for? Let's see if it worked."

They lay on the bed, stripped off their clothes, and kissed passionately. To his amazement, Brenner started to get aroused.

"It's working. I feel it," Jennie said. "Make love to me, darling."

This time Brenner did not fail. Jennie moaned and groaned with every movement. "You feel so good. Oh, this is fantastic."

While they both climaxed Brenner had to muffle a scream from Jennie. "Quiet. Martha will hear you."

"I don't care if the whole world hears me. I'm in ecstasy."

"I'm glad that I finally pleased you."

Jennie kissed his bare chest. "You sure did. Keep taking those pills, baby."

The next morning Jennie's face glowed when she sat down for breakfast.

"You look mighty radiant, Mrs. Sands," Martha said. "You must have rested well."

"Yes, I had a good night, real good." She smiled and rested her head on her hands while she hummed a song.

"You better stop your dreaming and eat your breakfast before it gets cold."

Brenner entered the dining room and sat opposite Jennie. "You look lovely this morning, my dear."

"Thank you." She giggled. "It's all your fault."

Brenner blushed and shook his head. He gobbled down his breakfast and started to leave.

He turned to his wife. "By the way, I'm declaring my candidacy for president today. You can watch me on television at noon."

"Wonderful. I wouldn't miss that for the world." Jennie kissed him goodbye. "Good luck."

Brenner had butterflies in his stomach all morning while he tried to work. He went over his notes concerning the issues many times. About an hour before they were to go on the air, he and Peter left for the television station.

The cameras were on him when Brenner said, "I am running for president this coming election as an independent candidate because I believe some drastic changes need to be made."

One of the newsmen yelled, "Have you picked a running mate?"

"Yes. It is this fine man next to me, Congressman Peter Johnston." He patted Peter's shoulder.

"What's you main goal?" asked another newsman.

"To make sure that everyone who is able to work has a job with ample wages to provide a good living." Brenner cleared his throat. "I also want to entice companies to return to this country so we have more jobs here. When this goal is met, the number of homeless and hungry people should be far less."

"How do you plan to accomplish this?"

"By giving the companies special tax breaks and by reducing government regulations."

A woman journalist asked, "Do you have a health care plan?"

"We're working on it," said Brenner. "When it is put together, we will let you know what it is."

Another man peered over his glasses. "What about people on social security? Will they continue to get their benefits?"

"Yes, and I'll ensure the money gets used only for their benefits, nothing else."

"Will retirement age stay the same or will you raise it?" asked an elderly newsman.

"I'd like to lower the optional age to 60 so that all young people have jobs, and those 60 and over can enjoy their lives. This plan is tentative and requires a great deal of research before it can be considered."

A thin man with shoulder-length hair and a youthful face raised his hand. "What are your views on crime?"

"One thing we should do is cut down on the amount of appeals allowed for convicted criminals. Three appeals and that's it. Too much money is wasted with the present system."

"How would you implement this?"

"Talk to the governors and hopefully get their support."

Brenner finished his interview and walked out the door, smiling. He went back to his office feeling satisfied with what had transpired.

Jennie greeted him with a hug when he arrived home around dinnertime.

"You were great, dear. You looked terrific on television, and you were so poised. I'm proud of you."

"Thank you."

Martha had chicken and dumplings ready for them. "I loved your answers to the questions from the press. You were wonderful, Mr. Sands."

"Thanks."

"Now both of you come eat your dinner while it's hot."

"We're coming," Brenner said.

"M-m-m-m...this is delicious," said Jennie.

Brenner rubbed his tummy. "You are the best cook in the whole world."

Martha turned red. "You are very kind. Thank you, Mr. Sands."

After watching a romantic movie on television, Brenner and Jennie went to bed. Once again, they made love.

"I'm so content that I don't crave a drink," Jennie said. "I told you sex is what I needed."

He kissed her forehead. "I am happy that I'm finally pleasing you."

"Oh, baby, you sure are satisfying me, a great deal."

Brenner knew that he had done the right thing by going to see Dr. Levin about his problem. The pills were working. Without them he would be a failure in bed.

Nothing could stand in the way of his becoming president now.

Chapter Twelve

Congress was on break.

Brenner took advantage of the time off and started his campaign. All of the campaign workers and their wives accompanied him. To make the trip easier, they rented a bus, provided with a driver, to travel the state.

The first state they went to was New Hampshire. They stopped in Concord and were greeted warmly by the governor, who surprised him with his endorsement.

Brenner addressed a large crowd. "I'm happy to be here today and announce that I'm running for president on the independent ticket. Your fine governor has given me his endorsement and I hope you will also give me your support."

The crowd broke out in loud cheers that lasted a few minutes. Brenner smiled and waved at them.

After the crowd quieted down, Brenner said, "I'd like you to meet my wife, Jennie, Peter Johnston, my running mate, and his wife, Peggy."

A man said to Jennie, "Do you think your husband would make a good president?"

"My husband would be a wonderful president," Jennie said. "He'll work very hard to get the job done."

"A woman yelled, "It is time for an independent president. I'm tired of the democrats and republicans. They all break their promises. We're ready for a change. Do you think you can do more to help the people?"

"I know I can, ma'am."

"I'm concerned about how crime has risen," a young man said. "Any ideas on how to slow it down?"

"One change would be to tighten up on paroles, especially for violent offenders. They should be behind bars for their full sentences."

People cheered and clapped.

"What about health care? Do you have a plan?" asked another woman.

"We're working on lowering the cost of insurance and doctors' fees so everyone can afford to buy insurance. This is possible with less government interference."

The crowd shouted, "Sands for president!" They held up signs with Brenner's name on them.

"What about us farmers?" asked a man dressed in overalls, a plaid shirt, and a straw hat.

"We'll ensure you get better prices for your goods. We would like to lower your interest rates for your machinery to run your farms. In exchange, you could give your excess produce to the homeless instead of wasting it."

"Sounds like we could work with you," the farmer said.

Brenner answered some questions about social security, assuring people that their benefits were safe if they elected him.

More cheers and louder clapping followed.

After answering a few more questions, Brenner said. "You're all invited to a get together in Liberty Hall, right around the corner. We are serving sandwiches, cake, coffee, and soft drinks. I can use volunteers for the campaign to work until election. I am hoping a lot of you will sign up and help our cause for a better country."

Hundreds of people showed up at the hall and many signed up to be volunteers. Brenner, Jennie, Peter, and Peggy mingled with the people and discussed issues. A couple of hours later they headed back to the motel.

Brenner collapsed across the bed. "This takes a lot of energy."

"I've still got some left," Jennie said. "Did you take your pill?"

"Give me a break, will you? I'm exhausted."

"Sorry. I thought we could release some tensions from a hectic day. I did not mean to upset you."

Brenner's voice softened. "I'm not upset, just tired. Come lay beside me and try to get some rest."

Jennie settled down alongside her husband and they soon dozed off, encircled in each other's arms.

They woke up a while later, took a hot shower, dressed, and met Peter and Peggy for dinner.

"What do you think of the responses of the people today?" asked Brenner.

"I thought they seemed very excited," Peter said. "Our chances seem good in this state."

"I agree," said Peggy. "I could feel the enthusiasm of the crowd. They showed they are ready for a change, an independent leader."

"What's next on the agenda?" asked Jennie with a smile.

"The governor invited all of us to have lunch with him, the lieutenant governor, some city officials, and their wives."

"That could help us get this state," said Peter.

"It should help a great deal," Brenner said. "We all have to answer their questions carefully. It wouldn't hurt to review our notes about the issues."

"Jennie and me, too?" asked Peggy.

"That would be a good idea, in case you are asked questions regarding what we stand for."

Jennie shrugged her shoulders. "We can handle it."

They enjoyed a delicious Maine lobster dinner, then shared some casual conversation. Jennie carefully took something out of her purse and slipped it in Brenner's hand. He blushed and when no one was looking, gulped down a little white pill with a glass of water.

Jennie patted his leg and smiled.

To top off the wonderful dinner, they enjoyed shortcake with fresh strawberries.

"It was worth the trip for this fantastic food," Peggy said.

Peter rubbed his belly. "I'll say. It was great. How about turning in while I can still move?"

They walked back to their rooms in high spirits. Once inside, Jennie unbuttoned Brenner's shirt and slipped it off. Next, she unzipped his pants and helped him step out of them.

"Your turn," Jennie said.

Brenner unzipped her dress and pulled it over her head. Her bra and panties slipped off easily. Jennie took her husband's hand and led him to the bed. She was in ecstasy when their bodies met and they made love.

"Oh, Brenner, you feel so good."

She fell asleep in her husband's arms, realizing that it was a long time since she had to call on her fantasy man.

They all met with the governor and city officials the following day. It was a huge success. Brenner answered all their questions to their satisfactions. Peter also impressed them. A few questions were directed to Jennie and Peggy and they responded in a gracious manner. Jennie's face beamed with the attention she received from the men and their wives.

When they headed back to the motel, Brenner grinned. "That definitely was a success. If the other cities go as well, New Hampshire is ours."

"This was the big one," Peter said. "The rest should be a piece of cake."

When they got back to their room, Jennie asked, "Where do we go from here?"

"The campaign workers, Peter, and I will make some quick stops in small towns. Just the guys are going this time. We will leave early tomorrow morning and return the next day."

Jennie pouted. "What am I supposed to do all alone?"

"Peggy will keep you company."

Jennie's eyes sparkled. "Maybe we could go shopping."

"That should keep you busy."

They went to bed early. Brenner and the rest of the guys left at 4 a.m. the following day, with plans to make whistle stops in several towns.

Peggy and Jennie met about 9 a.m. and had breakfast. Then they went to the mall and stopped at a shop that featured casual clothes.

"Look at these cute outfits," Jennie said. "I'm going to get a couple of skirts and blouses for traveling. Are you going to get something?"

"If I see an outfit I like," Peggy said.

Jennie and Peggy shopped until noon, then stopped at a small restaurant in the mall.

The waitress looked at Jennie. "Would you like a drink?"

"Yes, a martini, please."

She glanced at Peggy. "And you, ma'am?"

"A diet coke."

When the waitress left, Peggy glared at Jennie. "You're not supposed to drink. If Brenner finds out, he'll be furious."

"Brenner won't find out, unless you tell him. Will you?"

Peggy frowned and shook her head. "Why are you doing this? Things are going so good."

"I want a drink to celebrate the good things that have happened lately."

"Bad things can come from drinking, like in the past."

"You worry too much," Jennie said. "I know when to stop."

Peggy sighed. "I hope so. I don't want to get blamed for this."

"No one with blame you," said Jennie. "It's my choice. Come on. Have a drink with me. One won't hurt."

Peggy shook her head. "I gave it up for a while."

"Why? You don't have a drinking problem."

Her voice escalated a bit. "I don't want to drink, all right?"

"O.K.," Jennie said.

They browsed through a few more stores. When Peggy went to the ladies room, Jennie hurried into a small store, bought something, and put it in the bag with her clothes.

They left the mall and returned to the hotel about five o'clock.

"Want to grab a bite to eat?" Peggy asked.

"No thanks. I'm still full from lunch," Jennie said. "Do you want to visit with me for an hour or so?"

"Not tonight. I'm exhausted from all the walking. I think I'll go to my room and lay down."

Jennie nodded, waved goodbye to Peggy, and went inside her room. She ripped open the bag with the new clothes in it, and grabbed a bottle of scotch. She poured herself a drink, sat on the bed, and watched television.

The next thing Jennie remembered was Brenner hovering over her.

His eyes were filled with anger when he spoke. "I can't leave you alone for one night, can I?"

Jennie looked at him with blurred vision. "What are you talking about?"

Brenner waved an empty bottle of scotch in her face. "Why, Jennie? Why did you break your word?"

69

"I wanted to celebrate your reception here."

"Damn it...not that way. Did Peggy help you celebrate?"

"No. I was alone."

Brenner's lips quivered. "You told me that if we had more sex you would not need a drink. I guess that was proven wrong. What other excuses can you think of to drink?"

Jennie lowered her head while tears filled her eyes. "I'm sorry. I'll try harder from now. I promise."

"I don't believe you." Brenner paced, let out a deep breath, stopped and stared at Jennie. "Get dressed. I am notifying everyone that we are leaving early. I've got to get you home so Martha can keep an eye on you."

Chapter Thirteen

Martha greeted them at door a little before noon. She grabbed Jennie's suitcase. "It is wonderful having you home. The house was too quiet without you. Did you have a good trip?"

Jennie forced a smile. "Yes, ma'am."

Martha looked at Brenner. "Did you win the state?"

"It could not have gone better," Brenner said. "I think we won it."

"That's great news," said Martha. "I'll put your things away and fix you some lunch. It won't take long."

Brenner and Jennie freshened up and sat down to eat home made broccoli soup, sandwiches, and coleslaw.

"Good soup, don't you think?" Jennie said.

"Yes." Brenner frowned and continued to eat fast without looking at this wife.

"You are still angry with me, aren't you?" asked Jennie.

Brenner gazed at her. "More like, disappointed in you."

Jennie lowered her eyes. "I slipped once, but I won't again."

"I hope you mean that." Brenner stood up. "I'm going to the club to meet with the guys to plan our next trip for our campaign."

"Will you be long?"

"I should be home for dinner." He kissed her cheek. "Now you behave yourself while I'm gone."

"You have my word."

As soon as Brenner left, Martha appeared. "You didn't finish your lunch, Mrs. Sands. Don't you like it?"

"It's very good, especially the soup. I just can't eat any more."

"Can I get you some tea or coffee?"

"No thanks. That'll be all, Martha."

Jennie went into the den, turned on some soft music, and sat in a recliner. She started to read a contemporary love story and was soon intrigued with the book. A short while later she looked up and noticed Martha staring at her.

"Anything wrong?" Jennie asked.

Martha blushed. "No, ma'am."

"Then would you please leave?"

Martha nodded and went into another room. Jennie picked up her book again. After reading one chapter, her hands began to tremble. Jennie jumped up and searched every cabinet in the house, banging each door shut as she moved along.

When she reached the kitchen, Martha rushed in and gaped at her. "Can I help you find something?"

"No, just leave me alone."

"Sorry, ma'am, I'm only trying to help."

"You don't want to help," yelled Jennie. "You're spying on me so you can report my every move to my husband."

Jennie ran past Martha into her room. She tore off her clothes and took a shower, as hot as she could stand it. Her body felt calmer while she dressed into leotards. She approached her housekeeper.

"Sorry, Martha. I did not mean to be so nasty to you."

"I understand. Don't worry about it."

"I'm going to the spa for a couple of hours. That should make me feel more relaxed."

Martha got her keys. "Want me to drive?"

Jennie stared at her. "You're not going with me."

"You know what Mr. Sands said. You can't go anywhere without me. Now, am I going with you or do we stay home?"

Jennie frowned. "All right. You can drive me there, but you're probably going to be bored."

Martha moved quickly in and out of traffic and reached the spa in ten minutes.

"You drive like you have a hot rod," Jennie said.

"People do tell me I've got a heavy foot."

"Very heavy," said Jennie as they walked into the spa. She turned to Martha. "Since you will be coming with me all the time, why don't you join?"

"I'll watch for today," said Martha. "If I like what I see, I may join another time."

Jennie used the machines first, showered, changed into her bathing suit and plunged into the pool. She swam a couple of laps and felt a tug at her leg. Jennie stood up and gazed into the water. All of a sudden a young man emerged out of the water.

"Haven't seen you in a long time. Where have you been?"

Jennie's face reddened. "Hello, Randy."

He stood in front of her. "What happened to you? Why did you disappear?"

"The last time I went to your place I was greeted by a young beautiful girl."

"That must have been my sister."

"She was almost naked and did not act like your sister."

Randy lowered his eyes. "Forget about her. Let's go for a drink."

"I can't. I'm not alone." Jennie pointed to Martha who was staring at them from a bench.

"Who's that, your mother?"

"No, my housekeeper, and she is watching us. Don't get too close to me."

"What do you know, you have your own personal bodyguard."

"I can't talk with you now or ever again. Stay away from me or I'll report you for harassing me."

Randy gaped at her and shook his head.

Jennie moved far away from Randy and swam ten more laps. She got out of the pool, showered, and dressed.

Jennie walked up to Martha. "Ready to go?"

On the way home Martha asked, "Who was that handsome young man you were talking to?"

"An acquaintance."

"You'd better not let Mr. Sands see you with him. He would be jealous."

"I just bumped into him in the water. I hardly know him," Jennie said. "Will you please drop it?"

"Yes, ma'am."

They drove the rest of the way in silence. When they reached home, Brenner was waiting for them.

"Looks like you've been to the spa," he said. "Did you exercise too, Martha?"

"No, I watched for today. I may join another time."

Brenner kissed his wife's cheek. "What about you? Did you enjoy yourself?"

Jennie looked at Martha out of the corner of her eye. "It was invigorating."

Martha dashed into the kitchen and started dinner. An hour later, Jennie sat across from Brenner and enjoyed a delicious dinner.

"Looks like you behaved yourself today," Brenner said.

"How could I be bad? Martha watched every move I made."

"If you could be trusted you wouldn't need a companion."

"A jailer...she acts like a jailer to me."

Brenner stood up. "Let's go into the den and watch some television."

"Sounds good," She followed her husband into the room and sat close to him on the couch.

Brenner turned on a romantic movie and the hot love scenes soon caused Jennie to become aroused. She went to their room and slipped into an emerald-green nightgown.

When she rejoined her husband he gazed at her. "Wow! That gown looks sexy on you. Is it new?"

"Yes. I bought it in New Hampshire. Do you like it?"

"Very much."

They were quiet throughout the rest of the movie. Jennie edged closer to her husband. With a gleam in her eye she said, "Let's go to bed."

Brenner shifted his eyes from hers. "You go ahead. I'll be there as soon as the news is over."

Jennie lay on the bed anxiously waiting for Brenner. She realized that they had not made love since their last trip and hoped that they would tonight.

When Brenner got into bed, Jennie put her arms around him and pressed her body against his. "I want you so badly, darling."

He kissed her lightly. "Not tonight, Jennie. I've got to get up early. Peter, Rick, and I are going to make some quick stops in the rest of the New England states. We'll be gone for a couple of days."

"I can give you a great send off."

"Maybe when I get back."

Jennie pulled away from him. "You're using the trip as an excuse. What's the real reason?"

"That is the truth, and I didn't take my pill."

"Why not?"

"I forgot. I'll make it up to you when I get back. I promise."

"It seems I am always waiting for you for one reason or another."

With tears softly falling on her cheeks, Jennie moved further away from her husband and faced the wall.

The phone rang about eleven o'clock the next morning.

"Mrs. Sands, it's for you," Martha said.

"Hi, Peggy. Yes, please stop by this afternoon," Jennie said. "I'd love to have some company."

A couple of hours later Peggy entered the den and sat across from Jennie.

"Do you want some tea?" asked Jennie.

"Do you have orange juice?"

Martha brought Peggy juice and Jennie tea.

Jennie sat on the edge of her seat. "You said you had some wonderful news to tell me. I'm eager to hear it. What's the big news?"

Peggy grinned. "The rabbit died."

"You mean you're pregnant?'

"Yes. Isn't it great?"

Jennie hugged her. "I'm so happy for you. When did you find out?"

"This morning."

"I envy you." Jennie sighed. "We have been trying to have a baby for years but have had no luck."

"Did you ever think of adopting?"

"Brenner says no."

"Why?"

"He said that I don't have time for a baby because I have to help him with his campaign."

"Maybe he'll change his mind when the election is over," Peggy said.

"Hope you're right. Do you think I'd make a good mother?"

Peggy put her arm around Jennie. "You'd make a wonderful mother."

Jennie felt excited. "Does Peter know?"

"Not yet. He left before my doctor's appointment."

"I bet he will be thrilled when he finds out," Jennie said.

She looked at Peggy. "Let's go out to dinner and celebrate, right now."

"Sounds terrific," said Peggy.

"Do you mind if Martha comes?"

"Not at all."

On the way to the restaurant Martha said, "So you are going to be a mommy. Isn't that wonderful?"

"I couldn't be happier," said Peggy.

They arrived at the restaurant minutes later. Peggy ordered mostly vegetables and a large glass of milk.

"What did your doctor say today?" Jennie asked.

"I've got to be selective about what I eat, like what I have here." Peggy pointed to her plate. "He gave me a list of foods that are good for me and the baby. He also told me not to smoke nor drink alcohol. I don't smoke but I do enjoy an occasional drink. Of course, that's in the past. No more drinks."

Jennie peered at her. "Is that why you refused to drink on the trip? Did you think you were pregnant at that time?"

Peggy nodded. "I suspected it and didn't want to take a chance. That's why I ordered soda."

Jennie sighed. "You're pregnant. I can't believe it. Wish it were me."

Peggy patted her arm. "Your day will come."

"Hope you're right."

They got back as the sun was setting.

"Look at the sunset," Peggy said. "Isn't it brilliant tonight? I've never seen it so beautiful."

"The sky is celebrating your good news."

Peggy smiled. "How sweet."

"Do you want to stay with us tonight?" Jennie asked.

"Thanks but I'm going home. I'll be O.K."

"Want to go shopping for baby things tomorrow?"

"Sounds like fun," said Peggy. "Is 10 o'clock too early?'

"It's fine."

Jennie and Martha went inside the house a short time later.

"What a lucky woman," said Jennie. "I'm very tired. Think I'll got to bed."

"Goodnight, Mrs. Sands."

Even though Jennie was exhausted, sleep would not come. Thoughts of Brenner raced through her mind. She felt it would be wonderful to be pregnant with Brenner's child. Her insides ached for this miracle to happen.

She lay wide-eyed for hours, got up and paced the den and kitchen. Martha woke up and approached Jennie.

"Mrs. Sands, is anything wrong?"

"I can't sleep."

"Something's on your mind. Is it because you want a baby?"

"You're a smart woman."

"Maybe your doctor can help you," said Martha.

"Perhaps."

Martha heated something on the stove. "Here's a glass of warm milk. Drink it. It'll help you sleep."

"Thanks." Jennie gulped down the milk and went to bed. She fell into a deep sleep in minutes.

The phone woke her up. She peeked at her watch, 9 a.m.

"Hi, Jennie. How's everything going?"

"Brenner. I'm so happy you called. Things are great. Peggy spent the afternoon with me yesterday, and today we're going shopping." She hesitated. "Did Peter tell you the news?"

"Yes."

"Isn't it wonderful that Peggy is having a baby?"

"Terrific."

"I envy them, Brenner. I wish we were expecting."

"We'll discuss it when I get home."

Jennie took a deep breath. "How's the campaign going in New England?"

"Fabulous. Everyone is excited."

"That's great. When will you be home?"

"Tomorrow. I have to go now."

"Wait. I've got to ask you something. Do I have to take Martha shopping with us? Peggy will be with me."

"Yes, you must bring Martha. Remember what happened the last time you and Peggy went shopping?"

"All right. We'll take her."

"Good girl. See you soon."

Jennie hung up the phone and dressed for the shopping trip.

Peggy got there exactly at 10 o'clock.

"Brenner called a short time ago and said you told Peter about the baby," Jennie said.

Peggy's face glowed. "You're right. He did call last night and he's absolutely thrilled that we're having a baby."

"I am delighted for the both of you," said Jennie.

"Let's get going," Peggy said. "I can't wait to look at baby things."

Martha walked in long strides beside them on the way to the car. "Want me to drive?"

"No, thanks," said Jennie. "You're a hot rod driver. We don't want to shake up this baby." Jennie slid into the driver's seat.

They reached the mall in fifteen minutes. Peggy stopped in the stores that sold baby clothes. She held up on pink outfit. "Isn't this adorable?"

She seemed to be floating on a cloud as she viewed the clothes.

"Which one is your favorite?" asked Jennie.

She pointed to an aquamarine sleeper with teddy bears on it. Jennie paid for it. Martha bought her a soft, cuddly blanket that was covered with various pastel-colored angels.

"I can't let you two buy everything," Peggy said. She rummaged through a stack of nightgowns and purchased a couple of them.

"Do you need anything else?" Martha asked.

"I need everything," said Peggy. "This is my first baby and I don't have a thing."

"Let us buy more," Martha said. "What else can I buy for you?"

"Nothing, thank you. You're very sweet but I've got plenty of time. I don't want to buy everything in one day."

"Anyone getting hungry?" asked Jennie.

"I'm starved," Peggy said as she rubbed her tummy.

They found a small restaurant with a big salad bar. Peggy filled her plate twice.

"They have a large selection here," Peggy said.

"You're right. We'll have to remember this place," said Jennie.

They finished lunch and walked until they found a baby furniture store. Peggy pointed to many items she wanted.

"Get a couple of things," Jennie said.

"Not today. I want Peter with me for furniture. I'm only looking, but isn't everything beautiful?"

"Yes, Mrs. Johnston, and so are you," Martha said. "You're a beautiful mother. Isn't she, Mrs. Sands?"

Jennie's eyes became misty. "Yes, and very lucky."

They walked through the mall again.

"Mrs. Johnston, you'd better sit down and rest a bit," Martha said. "You should not overdo it."

"Don't worry. I feel wonderful. In fact, I never felt better in my life."

They came upon a cinema.

"Let's see what's playing," Jennie said.

Martha pointed to a movie about a young family. "Want to see that one? They all look so happy."

"I'd love to," said Peggy.

Jennie agreed and they entered the cinema. Two hours later they were on their way home.

"That was a terrific movie," Jennie said. "It was a heart warming story."

"Especially when Melinda had her baby," said Peggy. "Didn't she look happy?"

"We picked the right movie for you today," Martha said.

They reached Jennie's house. "Want to come in for a glass of milk?" Jennie asked.

"No, thank you," said Peggy. "I want to look at all my new things. Thanks for everything, you two. I had a great time today."

Jennie went into the house and slumped into a chair.

"Tired, Mrs. Sands?" Martha asked.

"A little."

"Mrs. Johnston is in high spirits, isn't she?"

"She sure is. Wish I were her," said Jennie.

Martha said, "Let me fix some dinner for you. Maybe you'll feel better."

"Just something small. I'm not too hungry."

After a light meal, Jennie went to her room, read more of her romantic novel, and fell asleep early.

She woke up with Brenner staring down at her.

"What time is it?" she asked.

"8 o'clock."

Jennie jumped up and hugged him. "Welcome home."

She got dressed and they had breakfast.

"Tell me about your trip," Jennie said.

"The people are ready for a change. They gave us a lot of support."

"So you may have New England on your side?"

"Looks that way."

Jennie sipped her coffee. "Was Peter excited when he heard the news about the baby?"

"Yes."

"Oh, Brenner. They are so fortunate. I'd love to have a baby."

He frowned. "We've been through this many times. We can't get pregnant. Can't you get it through your head?"

"Maybe the doctor who tested you years ago was wrong. See another doctor. He may have another opinion."

"No."

"We can adopt…"

"No."

"Why not?"

"We're too busy now with the campaign and all."

Jennie pouted. "So are Peter and Peggy and she is pregnant."

"I don't think it was planned. It happened naturally."

"Maybe that will happen to us some day."

"Perhaps, if you believe in miracles," said Brenner.

Chapter Fourteen

Brenner, Peter, and all of the campaign workers, and their wives, started another tour by bus. The first state they stopped in was Michigan. In Detroit they received a negative reception. Brenner stood on a platform and attempted to talk to the people. He introduced himself, Peter, and the wives.

"I am running for president as an independent and would like your support."

One man yelled, "I don't trust any politician, whether you're a democrat, republican, or independent."

"Yeah," said another man. "We've lost our jobs. What are you going to do about that?"

"I've got to study the situation, why you lost your jobs, and whether you can get them back."

"You can't do anything about our jobs," said a young man. "They've gone overseas."

"Another thing. You're always cutting money from the little people," said a husky man with long, dark hair. "Why can't you politicians cut your own salaries?"

Brenner nodded. "That's an excellent idea. If I am elected I plan to do that. I will start with my salary first."

"We don't believe you," said one woman. "You all make promises and break them once you are elected."

"Sorry you feel that way, but why don't you give me a chance? I am running because I want to change things."

"Go home," shouted an older man.

"Give the guy a chance," said a woman in the front row.

The crowd started jeering and shaking their fists in the air.

Brenner turned to the others. "Let's get out of here."

"What about the open house we planned?" Peter asked.

"With these people? Forget it. Let's move…fast."

They all dashed to the bus and climbed aboard.

"Get us out of here quickly," said Brenner to the driver.

"As soon as these people get out of my way," the driver said. "That mob looks angry. What did you say to them?"

"Nothing. They're furious at all politicians."

After about ten minutes the crowd moved out of the way. A couple of people threw eggs and tomatoes at the bus when it moved past them.

"Hope the next stop is friendlier than this," Peter said.

"Why are they blaming us for the loss of their jobs?" asked Jennie. "We had nothing to do with it."

Brenner sighed. "It's not us. Right now they hate all politicians because they are out of work."

Peggy leaned her head back. "Am I glad to be out of there."

"Are you all right?" Peter asked.

Peggy smiled. "Don't worry. I am fine. It doesn't hurt me to rush a little. The exercise will do me good."

"Well, this may be your last tour. I don't want to take a chance on anything happening to you or the baby."

Peggy put her head on her husband's shoulder. "You're worrying for nothing. I enjoy traveling with you."

"When we get back, you have to get a check up and ask the doctor if you can continue to travel."

"Yes, dear," smiled Peggy.

"Peter is right," Jennie said. "I was concerned about you, too. That mob was rough."

"All of you…enough already." Peggy put her head back and closed her eyes.

"Where do we go from here?" the bus driver asked.

"Look for a place to eat," Brenner said.

When they were out of the city of Detroit, they stopped for lunch. From there they made some quick stops in several smaller towns. The people were much friendlier and encouraging.

The bus left Michigan a few hours later and headed for Madison, Wisconsin. They rested for the night and met with a large crowd of people in the morning. Brenner presented himself, Peter, and their wives.

Brenner pointed to the crowd. "We're going to work for you."

Loud cheers filled the air. One man yelled, "I bet this independent can straighten out our country."

"I'll do my best," Brenner said.

They all answered questions for about an hour. From there they went to a hall for an open house. Many of the people signed up as volunteers to help with the campaign.

They proceeded to travel to smaller towns in Wisconsin where they stopped briefly and experienced warm receptions from the people.

The remainder of the tour consisted of stops in several mid-western states. For the most part, people greeted them with enthusiasm. The farmers were especially excited when Brenner proposed his plan for better prices on their products.

A week later they were on their way home. Everyone was tired but in a good mood.

"Except for Detroit, the tour went well," Brenner said.

"One unpleasant experience is not bad for all the stops we made," said Peter.

Jennie smiled. "Peggy and I met some very nice women, didn't we?"

"Yes," Peggy said. "They were friendly and eager to help."

"We'll take a few days off, try to unwind, then plan our succeeding trip," said Brenner.

Jennie yawned and stretched. "We can all use a break."

"Any idea where we are going next?" asked Peter.

"West, to the big states. Texas and California are crucial states to win."

"We've got to have a good plan for that tour," said Peter.

They arrived home in a few days. Martha greeted Brenner and Jennie with a big smile.

"It is good to have you home. How was your trip?"

"Great, but we are exhausted," Brenner said.

"How about some hot tea while I fix dinner for you?"

"Sounds wonderful," Jennie said.

While they were eating dinner, Martha said, "I saw you on television a few nights ago."

"Really, where were we?" Jennie asked.

"Detroit, Michigan. The people were nasty to you and it scared me. Did they hurt you?"

"Just our feelings," said Brenner. "The rest of the trip went very well. The people were terrific."

"Glad to hear it," Martha said. "And happy that you made it home safely."

Brenner and Jennie were in bed about an hour later.

"Feels good to be in our own bed," Brenner said.

"Sure does," said Jennie. She put her arm across Brenner's chest and fell into a deep sleep.

On Wednesday night the Aces High group met for their usual card game.

Chuck frowned. "Where's Raymond?"

"No idea," said Corey. "Has anyone seen him since we've been back?"

"No," said Brenner. "Maybe he has a date and he forgot about our meeting."

"No way. He hasn't dated in months," Chuck said. "I am going to call him." He walked to a pay phone.

"Raymond has never missed one of our games," Corey said. "I hope he is all right."

Chuck returned, shook his head, and sat down. "No answer."

"He can't answer if he is not home," Brenner said. "Let's try him later."

They continued their card game until eleven o'clock and started their campaign meeting.

"Our western tour will be the most important one besides New Hampshire," Rick said.

"California is the most critical state," Brenner said.

"Texas is significant, too," said Peter.

"What other states will we cover?" asked Corey.

"All the states we can, including Colorado and Utah," said Brenner. "We'll make quick stops in all the states going out there and the ones we missed coming back. We will stay longer in California and Texas."

"Time is running short for the election," Peter said. "Will we be able to get to all the states?"

"It'll be tight but we should hit them all," Rick said. "Two more trips ought to do it, including the south and mid-Atlantic states. Florida is a must."

"All of us will have to work on our issues more and be ready to convince the people that we are the best ones to vote for." Brenner. turned to Chuck. "Do you have anything ready on domestic issues?"

Chuck nodded and handed him some papers.

"Any questions on what you are to do?" Brenner asked.

Chuck scowled. "I'm too worried about Raymond. Can we try again?"

"Sit tight," said Brenner. "I'll try calling him."

A few minutes later, Brenner returned. "No answer. He must have gone away for a few days."

"Something must have happened," Chuck said. "It is not like Raymond to leave without telling someone."

"I'm sure there is nothing to worry about," said Peter. "I bet he will be home by morning."

"Hope you're right," Chuck said.

The meeting broke up and they all went their separate ways.

The next morning Brenner got a call from Chuck.

"I am really worried now," Chuck said. "Raymond is not answering his phone, and no on has seen him in two days. What the hell happened to him?"

"Calm down," Brenner said. "I am sure he's O.K."

Chuck took a deep breath. "I'm calling his landlord to check on him."

"If it makes you feel better." Brenner sighed and hung up the phone.

"Who was that?" asked Jennie.

"Chuck. He is up tight because Raymond has been missing for two days."

"Hope nothing is wrong."

"He probably went away for a few days with some woman."

"I doubt it. He would have told somebody," said Jennie.

"Perhaps she is special and he wanted to keep it a secret for a while."

"Maybe..."

"Feel like going out to lunch and doing some shopping?" Brenner asked.

"I would love it," Jennie said. "Give me a few minutes to freshen up."

Brenner peeked into the kitchen. "Martha, you don't have to fix lunch for us. Jennie and I are eating out."

"How nice," Martha said. "Have a good time."

They stopped in a cozy restaurant and enjoyed a seafood dinner. From there they went to a huge new mall and checked out many of their stores.

On the way back Jennie said, "Thanks. I needed that." She lay her head on his shoulder and closed her eyes.

Twenty minutes later they pulled into their driveway. Brenner pointed to a police car in front of their house.

"Hope it isn't Martha," said Jennie. She got out of the car and dashed into the house with Brenner behind her.

Detective Griffin was sitting in the den waiting for him. He stood up when they entered the room.

"What's happened?" asked Jennie.

"Raymond Masters was found dead in his apartment today."

Brenner scowled. "Unbelievable! How did he die?"

"We're not sure, but it seemed fishy to me."

"Fishy?" Brenner's eyes widened. "What do you mean?"

"We found a note next to his body."

"What did it say?"

"Two words…'my turn'. Would you know what he was trying to say?"

Brenner pondered for a few moments. "That's a mystery. I just know Raymond was despondent after Johnny's death, and always blamed himself for the accident." He bit his bottom lip. "Could he have taken his own life?"

"Possibly. Dr. Levin is doing an autopsy. We will know in a few days what killed him."

Jennie's face paled. "All these people dying. What's going on?"

"That's what I intend to find out," said the detective.

Chapter Fifteen

Another funeral...another dead politician.

Some relatives, close friends, along with many politicians, attended the service.

Detective Griffin approached Brenner outside. "I'd like to ask everyone some questions."

"Meet us at the club in an hour. It will be easier for us to talk there."

The members of the Aces High poker club walked into the room with long faces. Detective Griffin was waiting for them.

When they were seated, Chuck asked, "Do you know how Raymond died?"

"Dr. Levin has the results of the autopsy. Perhaps he can explain it better," said the detective.

"Raymond was drinking heavily," Dr. Levin said. "The cause of death was a mixture of alcohol and barbiturates."

"Why did he do such a stupid thing?" asked Corey.

"He came to see me a couple of days before he died and told me that he was still very depressed over Johnny's accident. He blamed himself for his death because he didn't react fast enough. I advised him to stop drinking and to seek therapy. As you can see, he did not listen to me."

"Did you prescribe the barbiturates?" asked the detective.

"No," Dr. Levin said.

"Did you prescribe any medicine to him?"

"No."

Detective Griffin tapped his pencil on the table. "Did any of you notice that Raymond was depressed or nervous any time before his death?"

"Why? Do you think he committed suicide?" asked Corey.

"I'm not sure. I only wondered if you noted anything unusual about his behavior."

"He seemed fine to me," Chuck said. "In fact, I did not see him drink that much."

Brenner pondered for a moment. "Raymond did drink a lot on our tours. He drank at night when our business was done. I found him drunk in his room one night and warned him not to behave that way again."

Detective Griffin looked at Corey. "Did Raymond drink much in front of you?"

"No more than usual."

"Anybody else observe strange behavior by Raymond before his death?"

"He often seemed depressed about Johnny's death," Rick said.

"You know how he died," said Peter. "Why all the questions?"

"Routine, gentlemen, just routine." He got up and left.

"Detective Griffin hinted that Raymond's death was not natural," Corey said. "He's got the autopsy report for proof. Does he suspect one of us killed him?"

"Your imagination is going wild again," said Brenner. "He's a cop. It is his job to ask questions."

"What is it with you, Corey?" Peter asked. "First you suggest suicide, now murder. Get out of your fantasy world. Raymond died from a mixture of alcohol and drugs. Case closed!"

Brenner took a deep breath. "Both of you, calm down. How about starting our trip to the western states in a couple of days? Maybe that will take our minds off this terrible tragedy."

"Great idea," Rick said.

Everyone agreed. A quick meeting was held with a discussion of their issues and a tentative plan for their journey.

Two days later the politicians and their wives were on route across country.

"I am kind of nervous with your taking this tour," Peter said to his wife.

Peggy's eyes shifted from his. "The doctor said that I am doing good and I can make the trip."

"This one is long and tedious."

"I feel great. Now stop worrying."

"I should have called him to confirm this. With Raymond's death and all, it slipped my mind."

"Believe me. I'm O.K.," said Peggy. "Don't I look good?"

"You look beautiful," Peter said. "I just don't want anything to go wrong with you or the baby."

"Peggy put her finger to his lips. "S-h-h-h-h."

Peter smiled and peered out the window.

They made quick stops in the states of Kentucky through Nevada. The people were excited and eager to help with the campaign.

The stop in California was longer. Huge crowds greeted them holding banners with the words, 'Sands for President, Johnston for Vice President.'

An elderly woman said, "You promised to make some necessary cuts to balance the budget. How are you going to do this? Will you cut social security and medicare?"

"No way. We will not touch social security or medicare. The first cut will be my salary, then the salaries of the rest of the administration, and congress. I also plan to have a committee study the pensions of congress and the administration in order to make reasonable reductions."

"I believe sacrifices should start from the top, with the government," said Brenner.

"Best idea I've heard yet," said a man, as he let out a loud howl.

"What about immigration?" asked another man. "Too many people are crossing the borders and draining the economy of California. What would you do about this?"

"I would recommend closing our borders for a while until we can get the situation under control." Shrieks emerged from the crowd.

Brenner continued. "I am not sure the courts will allow that so I've got some other alternatives. First of all, enforce the laws we have by sending back those that enter illegally. Also, stop the benefits for those coming in illegally. We must follow the laws for legal immigration and keep out illegal immigrants. If they don't have benefits to entice them, why would they come here?"

Loud cheers were heard.

Brenner raised his fist in the air. "No way should an American citizen go hungry and be denied medical care while an illegal immigrant is given medical assistance and other benefits instead of that American. Do you call this fair?"

"No...no," yelled the people. "Sands for president...Sands for president. He's our man."

After more speeches and loud cheering, they left for an open house. Hundreds of people were lined up to sign up as volunteers for Brenner's campaign.

They finished all the cities scheduled in California and stopped at a motel for some relaxation.

Before they exited the bus, Brenner said, "Our original plan was to go back home after California, take a break, and start our final trip. Anyone object to resting a couple of days then doing the remainder of the trip from here?"

"That's a great idea," Corey said. "That'll give us more time to plan for the election."

"It's not that far away," Rick said.

Peter looked at Peggy. "Feel up to it? If you're too tired you can fly home and be a lady of leisure until I get back."

"I won't hear of it," said Peggy. "I've never felt better."

"You do have circles under your eyes," Jennie said. "Aren't you sleeping well?"

"I sleep like a baby," smiled Peggy.

"All right. You can stay," Peter said. "But promise me if you get too tired, you will let me know and I'll arrange for you to go home."

"I promise."

After a break for two days and some fun in the sun, they started their final tour. They made a couple of quick stops and then a longer one in Texas, where people reacted warmly to Brenner and Peter. After a couple of days, they made short stops in other southern states, and arrived in Florida. The people there were as enthusiastic as in California. Bands played, banners flew, and people cheered. From Florida they made brief appearances in the other states and headed home.

Rick said, "This has been an exhausting but thrilling campaign, hasn't it?"

"It sure has. It has been a huge success," Peter said. "Hope it carries over to the election."

"'We are getting close to that time." Brenner held up crossed fingers in the air. "Victory is in our reach."

Jennie studied Peggy. The circles under her eyes appeared darker. "You'd better see your doctor when you get home."

Peggy smiled. "I will so you will stop worrying."

The bus sped along toward the outskirts of Washington D.C.

Chapter Sixteen

Brenner picked up the morning paper and read the headlines over and over, then grinned. "What a story. Take a look."

Jennie peeked over his shoulder. "The first independent to be elected. Terrific! How does it feel, Mr. President?"

She kissed his cheek and sat opposite her husband.

"I'm elated," Brenner said. "But you should not call me Mr. President until after the inauguration."

"Not even in the house?"

"I suppose so, if it makes you happy." Brenner pointed to her plate. "Eat your breakfast before it gets cold."

Jennie nibbled a small portion of food. "I am so excited. I can't believe this is all happening."

"It was close," said Brenner. "For a while I thought the democrats had it."

"You're right. That was fingernail biting time."

"Setting a record for votes by an independent was amazing. Agree?"

"Oh, yes. That was unbelievable," Jennie said.

Martha grinned from ear to ear while she strolled into the dining room with a pot of coffee and filled both cups. "Couldn't have happened to a finer couple. Congratulations."

"Thank you, Martha," Jennie said. "That is sweet of you."

Martha inspected her plate. "You have hardly touched your food, Mrs. Sands. Is something wrong with it?"

"No. It's my stomach. I've got too many butterflies."

"You have a right to feel that way," Martha said. "What a glorious day." She left the room humming.

Jennie pondered for a moment. "Let's go somewhere and celebrate your victory."

"Where?" asked Brenner. "We will be swarmed by people anywhere we go."

Her eyes twinkled. "We could rent a private boat, cruise and just relax. Sound good?"

"I kind of like that idea," Brenner said. "Call to see if you can make arrangements."

Fifteen minutes later Jennie scampered into the den. "Can you be ready in an hour?"

They were about to leave when Martha appeared with a cooler.

"What's in there?"

"Sandwiches, goodies, and soft drinks. You'll get hungry on the water."

"You think of everything," Jennie said. "Thanks."

Martha waved to them as they walked toward the car. "Have a good time."

When they boarded the cabin cruiser, a man in his forties greeted them. "I'm Captain Hanson. Welcome."

"We're Brenner and Jennie Sands." Brenner glanced quickly around the area and saw no one else.

The captain gaped at Brenner and shook his hand. "Pleased to meet you, Mr. President."

"I'm still Senator Sands until January," said Brenner. "But we would appreciate our privacy. Is anyone else here?"

"No, sir. You have the boat all to yourselves, except for me." The captain smiled. "It's a pleasure to have you aboard. Follow me. I will give you a tour of the boat."

First, Captain Hanson showed them the deck, and from there, they went below and viewed a spacious room equipped with a full-sized bed, a bar, and an oak dining set. Huge fishing poles and nets were attached to the light wood paneling. An aquarium, located along another wall, had hundreds of multi-colored tropical fish swimming around inside.

"Is this our room?" asked Jennie.

"Yes. Do you like it?"

"This is fantastic. Right, Brenner?"

"Very nice."

"I've got to start the engines," the captain said. "If you need anything, call me from that phone on the bar."

Brenner and Jennie changed into bathing suits and headed for the deck. They reclined on lounge chairs that faced the water and closed their eyes. The sun shone through puffy white clouds and warmed up their bodies while the boat cruised along the soft waves.

Jennie handed Brenner some lotion. "Put some of this on. You could get a bad burn today."

Brenner covered his body with the lotion then lay back and closed his eyes. "This is great. Haven't been this lazy in months."

Jennie whispered in his ear. "Take a pill today?"

Brenner jumped up and stared at her. "You expect me to make love to you on this deck?"

"Wouldn't it be exciting?"

"For God's sakes, Jennie. What about the captain and the boats going by?"

"The captain's occupied and a boat has not passed us since we have been out here."

Brenner scowled. "We're not making love here."

"How about in the cabin?"

"Forget it."

"Did you take your pill?"

"No. Now let me relax, will you?"

Jennie laughed. "You should try something wild for a change. Maybe you would like it."

Brenner blushed, put headphones on, and listened to classical music with his eyes closed. Jennie picked up a sexy novel and escaped into another world where the man focused on pleasing the woman while she in turn satisfied him. She visualized Brenner being that man and she the woman.

"From the smile on your face it must be a good book," Brenner said.

"It is wonderful."

"Are you getting hungry?" asked Brenner.

"A little. I didn't have much breakfast."

Brenner stood up. "Let's go to our room. We should get out of the sun for a while."

Jennie's eyes lit up.

"Don't get any ideas. The answer is still no."

They got into comfortable clothes and ate some of the food Martha had packed for them.

Jennie peered at her husband. "Will you take a pill please?"

"I guess that is the only way you will stop bugging me."

Brenner searched every corner of his suitcase. "Sorry. I can't find them. I guess I left them home."

"Damn," Jennie said. "You must have done that intentionally."

"I swear that is not true. I packed in a hurry and thought I had them."

"It's been such a long time since we have been intimate, and I'm ready."

Brenner frowned. "You know how busy we've been."

"We've got some time to relax now. Could you try it without the pill?"

"All this talk isn't helping me be calm."

"Would you respond better if I talked less?"

"Probably," said Brenner.

"One question and I'll drop the subject."

"I'm afraid to ask. What?"

Jennie took in a deep breath and exhaled. "Promise me that you will take a pill when we get home."

"I promise. Now can we enjoy the rest of the day?"

"I will do my best to be good," smiled Jennie.

They stayed in the room during the hottest part of the day and went back on the deck for a short time, while the boat headed toward shore.

Jennie gazed into the water. "Do you think there are sharks in there?"

"Maybe."

"If I were swimming in that water and a shark came close to me, what would you do?"

"I would save you," Brenner said.

Jennie shook her head. "You would let him devour me to get rid of me."

Brenner laughed. "Not a bad idea."

Jennie glared at him. "You mean that, don't you?"

"Of course not. What would life be without you, my dear?"

"Kind of dull, I guess."

"Very dull. Now get changed. We'll be docking soon."

On the way back home Jennie asked, "It was fun, wasn't it?"

"Yes. We'll have to try it again before the inauguration, maybe with Peter and Peggy."

"I don't know about Peggy. She is kind of far along."

"We'll see how she feels."

They got back, showered, and had supper.

"You two look red as lobsters," Martha said. "Hope you didn't get too much sun."

"Looks worse than it is," said Jennie. "I put plenty of lotion on and it doesn't hurt. What about you, Brenner?"

"I feel fine."

Jennie stretched and yawned. "I'm a little tired. Bed sounds good about now. Coming, dear?"

"I'll be there soon."

Jennie put on a slinky black teddy and climbed under the covers. About ten minutes later, Brenner was beside her.

"You not only look sexy, you smell great," he said.

"Did you…"

He put his fingers to her lips. "Yes, I took it. Now let us see if it worked."

Jennie felt that Brenner was forcing himself to please her. They made love but the spark seemed gone, even for her.

Chapter Seventeen

Jennie dialed the phone. "Peggy, are you up to shopping?"

She showered, put on a comfortable dress, and approached Brenner in the den.

"Peggy and I are going to the mall to shop for gowns for the Ball."

Brenner looked up from the book he was reading. "Got enough money?"

"I think so. If not I'll use plastic."

"Have fun."

Jennie kissed his cheek and left. She picked up Peggy ten minutes later and caught a glimpse of her pale face and the circles under her eyes. "How are you feeling?"

"A little tired but otherwise good," Peggy said. "Hope I find a gown to cover this huge body."

Her hands patted her stomach gently.

"You are tiny for seven months. I'm sure you will fit into something pretty."

Peggy smiled. "I hope so."

After going into a couple of stores, Peggy sat on a bench.

"Are you all right?" asked Jennie.

"I have to catch my breath. I tire easily."

"If this is too much for you, I will take you home."

"No, I won't hear of it." Peggy stood up. "I am O.K. now."

They went into a few stores with Peggy resting at intervals. None of the gowns were appealing to them.

"Hungry?" Jennie asked.

"Starved."

After eating a healthy lunch, they headed for home.

"At least we have an idea what is in fashion," said Jennie.

"I was not crazy about anything we saw. What about you?"

"No. It looks like our gowns will have to be custom made."

"Mine will have to be made extra large, with room to grow," laughed Peggy.

"I'll make some phone calls and make an appointment as soon as possible," said Jennie. "You'll only have to go to one place and won't have to walk so much."

Peggy shrugged her shoulders. "It was not that bad today."

Jennie pulled up in front of Peggy's house. "When do you see your doctor again?"

"Tomorrow."

"Don't forget to tell him how tired you get."

"Stop worrying. I'm fine." Peggy waved and went into the house.

The following week Francois measured Jennie and Peggy for gowns. He assisted them in choosing appropriate material for each.

"Does this stretch?" asked Peggy.

"Don't worry, my dear," Francois said. "I'm taking your condition into account. I'll leave room for you to grow."

After several fittings and a month later, the women returned for the final fitting. Peggy viewed her reflection in the mirror with satisfaction. Her sapphire-blue gown flowed loosely over her hips to a couple of inches from the floor. Rhinestones were embedded on top of the gown. She pulled the sides out, smiled, and twirled in a full circle.

"You look gorgeous," said Francois.

"You do," Jennie said. "You'd never know that you are pregnant."

Jennie slipped her gown on and studied herself in the full-length mirror. The satin gown was off-white with pearls woven throughout it. She nodded and grinned. "I don't think any more alterations are necessary."

"It's perfect, and you are beautiful," Francois said.

"I agree," said Peggy. "You are going to turn all their heads at the Ball."

Jennie drove carefully down the busy highway. "I am so happy with our gowns. Francois did a wonderful job."

"I agree. I love them. I can not wait to show Peter."

When Jennie pulled into her driveway, Brenner's car was missing. She found Martha in the kitchen fixing dinner.

"Did Brenner say where he was going?"

"He said to tell you he was going to the Aces High Club to play cards and he wasn't sure when he would be back."

Meanwhile, Brenner drove to a motel about twenty miles from the highway. He pulled his hat down to the rim of his dark glasses and walked with long strides to the room. Bunny lay naked waiting for him on the bed.

"Did anyone recognize you?"

"No," said Bunny. "I wore a disguise."

"Good."

"You know, this is getting risky," Bunny said.

"You're right but I had to be with you." He stripped his clothes off and rushed into Bunny's waiting arms. They made love until their bodies collapsed from exhaustion.

The key carefully turned in the lock and Brenner tiptoed into the house. He slipped into bed beside Jennie.

"You've been playing cards this long?" asked Jennie.

"We had a meeting about the upcoming term and got long winded."

"Sounds fascinating." Jennie gave him a peck on the cheek and rolled over.

During breakfast Jennie looked at Brenner with a twinkle in her eye. "Let us do something different."

"Do I dare ask? What?"

"How about visiting our parents and relatives?"

Brenner pondered for a moment. "That's a good idea. We have more than one month before the Ball, then we'll be too busy."

Two days later they were on their way to Connecticut.

As they rode along Rt. 95 in a limousine driven by a secret service agent, Jennie said, "Our gowns are done."

"Are you satisfied?" asked Brenner.

"Yes, Peggy and I both love them." Jennie frowned. "But I am worried about Peggy. She is so tired all the time."

"That's normal for being pregnant."

Jennie shook her head. "Not that tired. Hope she goes full term with no complications."

"I am sure she will."

The traffic was heavy from Washington D.C. through New York but dwindled when they entered Connecticut.

Brenner peered out the window. "The trees are bare and getting ready for winter."

"They are prettier in the fall with their brilliant colors," said Jennie. "It's my favorite time of year."

The other agent seated next to the driver turned and asked, "What's the name of the town we are looking for?"

"Mystic," said Brenner. "You will see a sign soon."

A short time later they turned off the highway. A few miles down the road, they pulled on to a circular driveway that led to a gigantic white colonial home with black shudders. Brenner's parents welcomed them and he gave his mother a big hug.

Brenner felt tense when his father hugged him. A scene from years ago of his father in bed with a young boy flashed before him. His whole body shuddered.

"Are you all right?" asked his father. You're trembling."

"I'm fine. Just felt a little chill."

His mother gazed at the other men. "You brought friends with you? How nice."

"They're sort of like our bodyguards," said Brenner.

Mrs. Sands clasped her hands and grinned. "How exciting!"

"Our son is going to be president, dear. He gets special treatment now," said Brenner's dad.

Mr. Sands put an arm around Brenner's shoulder and pulled Jennie near him. "You are special too, sweetheart."

They went into the house and were led to their rooms by the housekeeper. After unpacking, everyone gathered in a room with large windows overlooking the water that softly hit the beach.

"What a magnificent view," said one of the agents.

"This is my favorite room," Mrs. Sands said. "When I want to relax, I come here."

The housekeeper appeared and served tea and small desserts to all.

"Thank you," said Mrs. Sands. "That'll be all for now."

Mr. Sands gazed at Brenner and smiled. "What a thrill it was when we learned you won the election."

"How does it feel to be president?" asked Mrs. Sands.

"I am not president yet, Mom."

"You will be soon. Are you excited?"

"It hasn't sunk in yet. Maybe once I am sworn in and start making decisions, it will hit me."

Jennie sipped her tea. "It's great sharing this time with you, Mom and Dad, and having the opportunity to unwind."

Brenner nodded. "In another month we will be very busy."

Jennie looked at her mother-in-law. "Would you mind if Brenner and I walked on the beach?"

"Not at all. Go before it gets dark."

"Let's wait," Brenner said.

Jennie stood up and grabbed his hand. "Come on."

They walked close to the water, hand in hand. Jennie glanced behind her and saw two figures.

"Can't we do anything without those clowns following us?"

"Get used to it," Brenner said. "It will be worse when we get to the White House."

Jennie yanked off her shoes and stepped into the water. She cupped some water in her hands and threw it at Brenner.

"Hey! What are you doing? That water is cold."

"You don't know how to have fun," laughed Jennie.

"Get out of the water before you catch cold."

Jennie strolled back on to the beach and put her arm through Brenner's. "I'll stay out of the water but I'm keeping my shoes off. The sand feels good between my toes."

Brenner frowned. "Remember to put them back on before you go back into the house."

"Yes, sir."

They returned in time for an appetizing dinner. In the early evening some of Brenner's relatives visited and extended their congratulations and best wishes for his presidency.

Louise E. Ducharme

Four days later, they headed for Old Saybrook, Connecticut.

The limousine parked in front of a gray cape-cod house, smaller than the one they just left. Jennie's mom and dad greeted them warmly and led them inside. Mr. Cooper motioned for them to follow him to the den. Pictures of various types of ships and fishing scenes were displayed on the walls. An aquarium, built into the wall, contained large goldfish and numerous other colorful fish. Comfortable plaid furniture was placed around the room with a round braided rug in the middle. Warm air was felt from a crackling fire in a stone fireplace.

Mrs. Cooper entered the room with coffee and pastries. She served Brenner first. "I'm proud of you son."

"Thanks, Mom."

"Dear, you will be First Lady. How does it feel?"

"Great. I'm walking on a cloud," Jennie said.

Mr. Cooper addressed Brenner. "How about a little fishing?"

"Sounds wonderful," said Brenner. "I haven't fished in a long time."

Mr. Cooper and Brenner left and fished off a dock in back of the house. The two agents followed them.

Jennie sighed "Happy to be alone with you, Mom. Those agents were getting on my nerves."

She and her mom talked non-stop until the men returned. Brenner grinned while he held up two huge trout.

The last days of their vacation came quickly to an end. Brenner and Jennie left for home, optimistic of good days ahead.

Chapter Eighteen

All eyes gazed at Brenner and Jennie when they walked into the room.

"What a handsome couple," said a female guest to her husband.

Brenner's ten-pound weight loss was revealed in the dark tuxedo he wore. His brown hair, streaked with gray, brushed his forehead which made him appear younger that his forty-six years.

Jennie looked captivating in her white beaded gown that outlined her body perfectly. Stars sparkled throughout her auburn hair that swerved back in a French twist.

Peter and Peggy walked arm in arm behind them. Peter, a handsome man with black wavy hair and piercing green eyes, and Peggy, radiant in her blue gown, smiled to the crowd.

Everyone in the room stood, clapped, and cheered as they made their way to their seats.

"Pinch me," Brenner said. "I must be dreaming."

"Isn't this exciting?" said Jennie. "We made it to the Inaugural Ball. I can't believe it."

Peggy nodded. "Our hard work paid off."

"You look beautiful," Jennie said. "Do you feel as good as you look?"

"I feel great."

Peter took Peggy's hand. "I'm keeping a close eye on her so she doesn't over do it."

"Good."

Lots of speeches followed with Brenner speaking last. He was interrupted at intervals with loud cheers.

A fantastic dinner was served. After the tables were cleared, the band started playing. Brenner took Jennie's hand and led her to the dance floor. A gigantic chandelier above them reflected images from the stars on Jennie's hair on to the ballroom floor.

"You are a gorgeous woman," Brenner said.

"And you're my prince charming," smiled Jennie.

Peter and Peggy waltzed by them.

"Do you think Peggy should be dancing?" asked Jennie.

"Why not?"

"She may hurt herself."

"Nonsense. You worry too much."

They sat down and Jennie excused herself to go to the ladies room. On the way back, she glanced to see if Brenner was watching her. When he looked the other way, she stopped at a punch bowl.

Brenner got suspicious after she left the table several times during the evening. "Are you drinking?"

"Me?" giggled Jennie. "Of course not."

Brenner took her arm. "Let's get some coffee."

Jennie stopped at a table and pointed. "See. That is what I have been drinking, harmless punch."

Brenner walked up to a waiter. "Can you tell me what is in that punch?"

"Fruit juices, vodka, gin, and rum," the man said. "Why? Is something wrong with it, sir? Do you want us to make another one?"

"No. That won't be necessary."

Brenner moved with long strides back to Jennie, grabbed her hand, and led her into a side room. He looked around to ensure no one was there.

"So, you have been drinking harmless punch, have you? Next you are going to tell me you don't know what's in it."

Her eyes shifted away from his. "Same as all punches, fruit juices."

"You knew there was liquor in it. That is why you kept going back." He threw his arms up in the air. "Why, Jennie? Why are you doing this to me...to us?"

She shrugged her shoulders. "I thought a little bit would not hurt."

"You are looking tipsy to me, Peter, and Peggy. Wonder how many others have noticed?"

She smirked. "Want me to go home?"

"No. That would be too obvious. You drink coffee until you are sober. And no more punch or liquor. Understand?"

She saluted and laughed. "Yes, sir."

"It is not funny, Jennie. This is our future you are playing with."

Her eyes were downcast. "I'll be good. Honest."

"To make sure you stay that way, you go nowhere without an escort. Peggy, Peter, and I will take turns."

With her hands on her hips and her chin protruding, Jeannie said, "Are you and Peter going to follow me into the ladies room?"

"Of course not. We'll wait outside."

"I feel like I am in prison."

"You chose to drink, now you pay the consequences."

"What if everyone drinks around me?"

"You drink coffee."

"All right. You win," Jennie said.

"We must go back. Take a hold of my arm and walk as if nothing happened," said Brenner.

They passed Chuck Andrews on the way back to the table. "Where have you two been? Thought you left."

"No. We were just fooling around a bit," Jennie said.

98

Brenner turned crimson. "Hush."

"You're a lucky guy," laughed Chuck.

"Real lucky." Brenner hastened his steps with Jennie trying to keep up.

"Lighten up," she said. "Why can't you ever have fun?"

"This is not a fun event," Brenner said in a low voice. "Stop behaving like a fool. Why can't you act like a First Lady?"

"For a while I did forget what role I was playing. Guess I will have to try to be more like you."

"You are impossible," Brenner said.

He took her hand, led her back to their seats, and ordered two coffees.

Peter looked at Brenner. "Is everything O.K.?"

Brenner nodded. "The situation is under control."

"You missed some great music," Peggy said. "We've been dancing our feet off."

"Did your doctor give you permission to dance that much?" Jennie asked.

"I don't need his permission. Dancing is good for me."

"I tried to talk her out of it, but she threatened to dance with other guys if I refused her." Peter grinned.

The band started to play a jazz number. Peggy stood up and grabbed Peter's hand.

"See what I mean?" Peter said.

"Dance very slowly, please," said Jennie as she drank her coffee.

"She's being too risky," Brenner said.

"I agree," Jennie said. "Peggy should be more careful. This music is too fast."

Half way through the song, Jennie pointed to the dance floor. "Look!"

Peggy and Peter stopped dancing and Peggy rushed to the ladies room.

"Something is wrong," Jennie said. "I've got to check on her."

"I'm coming with you," Brenner said.

She dashed to the ladies room and found Peggy holding on to the sink. A lot of blood was visible around her feet.

Jennie gasped. "Oh, my God! Don't move, Peggy. I'll get help."

"I should have listened to you," sobbed Peggy.

"Sh-h-h-h—try to save your strength."

Jennie banged the door behind her and ran to Brenner. "Call 911, and hurry!"

"What happened?"

"Peggy's hemorrhaging."

Jennie went back inside and put her arms around Peggy. "Help is on the way. Try to be calm."

In minutes paramedics carried Peggy on a stretcher to an ambulance. Peter rode with her and held her hand.

"Is there any hope?" Peter asked a paramedic.

The paramedic shrugged his shoulders. "She lost a lot of blood."

Peter squeezed Peggy's hand. "Please, God, save my wife and our baby."

Peter hung his head and wept.

The emergency room staff was waiting when they arrived. The doors flew open and Peggy was whisked into a trauma room. Six people huddled around her and worked in unison to stabilize her.

Blood was drawn from one arm while a blood pressure cuff was wrapped around the other arm and inflated. Electrical leads that were attached to circular patches were taped to her chest. One of the staff listened to Peggy's heartbeat, then the baby's.

Someone arrived with blood and injected it into her. The team worked frantically to save them.

Peter paced outside the trauma room. One of the staff opened the door and raced by.

"How is she?" Peter yelled.

The staff member shook his head.

"Peter, come sit down with me and Jennie," Brenner said.

Peter plopped into a seat with his head in his hands. "Lord, help Peggy, please."

Brenner held one of his arms and Jennie held the other. They prayed together.

A couple of hours later a doctor appeared. "How's my wife?" Peter asked.

"She's still alive," said the doctor. "But her condition is very critical. We should know by morning if she will make it."

After the doctor left, Peter said, "Brenner, why don't you and Jennie go home? There's nothing you can do."

"What about you?" Jennie asked.

"I'm staying," Peter said. "I won't sleep anyway."

The only figure that could be seen in the waiting room was Peter pacing. He finally sat down when his legs were ready to collapse. Fifteen minutes later his head slumped forward and he was snoring.

A streak of light streamed through the blinds and rested on Peter's eyes. He jumped and peered at his watch. It was six a.m. The door to the trauma room burst open and the doctor walked with long strides toward Peter.

"Is she O.K.?" Peter asked.

The doctor nodded. "She made it."

Peter smiled and shook his hand. "Thank, God. That is great news. Is the baby all right?"

"The baby is fine."

Peter sighed. "Can I see my wife?"

"Not until she is moved into a private room, in about an hour."

Peter made a phone call. "Brenner. Peggy and the baby made it. Isn't that wonderful?"

After Peggy was moved, Peter visited her.

Her eyes were misty. "I was stupid, wasn't I?"

"I guess all that dancing was risky," Peter said. "But the important thing is that, thank God, you're all right."

He kissed her and ran his hand over her belly. "And the little one is all right."

Her doctor entered the room and checked Peggy.

"When can she go home?" Peter asked.

"Tomorrow. But she must go straight to bed and stay there until the baby is born. Any extra activity can be dangerous to her and the baby."

Peggy laughed. "That means no more dancing?"

"That's right. And you, Mr. Johnston, must ensure that she stays in bed."

"I'll make sure she is watched, day and night."

Peter left the hospital weary but feeling lighter. Peggy was brought home the following day.

For two weeks Peggy lay in bed, except to use the bathroom.

One evening Peter peeked in the room. "How is the lady of leisure?"

"Very bored," Peggy said. "I'm getting tired of reading and television."

"What would you like to do?"

"Have this baby."

"One more month and you'll have the baby."

"That's too long," Peggy said. "Could you help me up, please? I have to use the bathroom."

A few minutes later Peter heard a scream. He yanked the bathroom door open and found Peggy standing in a pool of blood.

The ride in the ambulance seemed longer this time. Peter questioned if Peggy would survive another massive blood loss.

Peggy was rushed into a trauma room. Several people surrounded her, took her vital signs, and monitored her heart.

"She's in shock. Call Code-99," one member said.

The hospital paging system came to life in seconds. "Code-99, shock-trauma unit, Code-99…"

A doctor, and some nurses took over and worked on Peggy. More blood was put into her body.

Peter was too tired to pace. He squeezed the hands of Brenner and Jennie, leaving his nail prints in their palms.

"I don't want to lose her," Peter said.

"I'm sure she will pull through," said Jennie. She glanced at Brenner and shook her head.

The trauma door opened and the doctor appeared. Peter ran to him with a twinge of hope in his eyes. "She made it, right?"

A frown crossed the doctor's forehead while he put a hand on Peter's shoulder. "Sorry, Mr. Johnston. She's gone."

"No...no," yelled Peter. "I don't believe you. What about the baby?"

"Your son is dead, too."

Peter threw his hands up in the air. "It can't be true. God, you were supposed to save them. Where were you?"

Jennie and Brenner hurried to his side and took his arms right before Peter's legs collapsed.

On the way home Peter stared into the darkness and wondered how he could face this devastating loss.

Peter was hesitant to look at Peggy and his son who was beside her in a little casket. His mom and dad knelt in front of them and prayed.

They approached Peter and hugged him. "Peggy was so beautiful. And the baby, too."

They sobbed and walked away. Peter stared straight ahead with tears streaming down his cheeks.

The lines were endless. He didn't realize they had so many relatives and friends. Before the bodies were taken to the cemetery, he kissed Peggy and his son good-bye.

After the ceremony was completed and most of the people gone, Peter stared at the fresh grave site with his legs frozen in place.

Jennie nudged him. "Come on, Peter. You can't stay here."

She took his arm and led him to the car. Peter put his head on Jennie's shoulder and let go of his pent up emotions. She took a handkerchief and wiped his face and hers.

"Remember, Peter. I will be there whenever you need me."

Brenner glanced at Jennie and frowned.

Chapter Nineteen

Peter buried himself in work to help cope with his loss. His new position as vice president offered him many challenges. The first promise that he attempted to fulfill from his campaign concerned crime. He met with various law enforcement officers, judges, and lawyers to determine what could be done to lower the crime rate and ensure that violent offenders stay behind bars. Long hours were spent studying the topic.

One evening he arrived home about nine o'clock and found Jennie waiting for him.

"This is a pleasant surprise," Peter said.

"I'm checking up on you," said Jennie. "You're looking better than the last time I saw you. How are you doing?"

"Work helps me forget, until I get home. The house is so empty without Peggy." Peter's eyes grew misty.

"That's why I am here, to keep you company."

The housekeeper brought in his dinner. "Bring a plate for Jennie, please."

"I've already eaten."

"Please, have a little so I won't have to eat alone."

Jennie nodded and smiled. "How's your job going?"

"It keeps me busy which is what I need."

After a couple of hours, Jennie peeked ht her watch. "It's getting late. I must get home."

"Does Brenner know you are here?"

"No. I left before he got home."

Jennie tiptoed into the house and started to walk past the den.

"Hey. Where have you been?" Brenner asked. He put down the notes he was reading.

"Peter's."

"What for?"

"To check up on him," Jennie said.

"Is he doing better?"

"A little. Nights are his hardest times. That's why I plan to stop there every night until he feels stronger."

Brenner stared at his wife. "Are you doing anything besides talking?"

"Of course not," said Jennie. "I'm helping him through his grief."

"I took a pill tonight. Want to help me feel better?"

Jennie followed him to their room, undressed, and lay next to her husband. She tried to get aroused but felt lifeless.

"Sorry," Jennie said. "I'm exhausted."

"Is it easier to satisfy Peter?" Brenner turned away in frustration.

"Nothing's going on with Peter and me. We're just friends."

"If that is true, stop going over there."

"Not until I know he will be able to cope alone."

Jennie sat up. "I can't believe you're so jealous of Peter."

Brenner hesitated. "I'm not jealous, but it is not right for you to be going there alone."

"Why don't you come with me?"

"No. I'm too busy."

"How about Peter coming here for dinner every night?"

"Maybe two or three times a week. That's it."

Jennie invited Peter for dinner the following night. He left work early enough to be there by seven o'clock. Brenner and Peter discussed some points of the crime issue.

Jennie helped clear the table. Martha said, "Mrs. Sands, you don't have to do that."

"It's better than talking politics."

Martha laughed. "Know what you mean, ma'am."

About an hour later, Peter got up to leave. "Thanks for having me for dinner. I appreciate your thoughtfulness." He looked at Martha. "And your cooking was great as usual."

"Glad you liked it, sir," Martha said.

"Since you enjoyed it so much, how about sharing dinner with us day after tomorrow?" asked Jennie.

"Is it all right with you, Brenner?"

"Of course."

"Thanks. See you Friday."

The next evening Jennie approached her husband. "I'm meeting Nikki Brown at the spa. I haven't gone anywhere since Peggy died."

"It will do you good to get out," Brenner said.

Ten minutes after she left Brenner made a phone call. "Can we meet tonight for a couple of hours?'

"No," said Bunny. "We can't see each other anymore."

"Why not?" Brenner asked.

"Too many people are watching us now. Our reputations are at risk."

"I need to see you, please. I will be careful."

"Sorry..." The phone clicked in Brenner's ear.

His hands trembled while tears fell softly on his cheeks.

Meanwhile, one of the secret service agents accompanied Jennie to an elite health center for members of the congress and their wives.

Jennie found Nikki riding an exercise bike and sat on one beside her.

"Been waiting long?" Jennie asked.

"Just got here."

"I had to get out tonight," Jennie said. "I have not done much after Peggy's death."

"That was a shock," Nikki said. "How's Peter doing?"

"It's going to take time for him to heal."

"Probably the best thing for him would be to remarry in the near future," said Nikki.

"I don't think he'll get married for a while. It would take a very special woman to take Peggy's place," said Jennie.

"That's for sure," Nikki said as she got off the bike. "Come on. Let's try the pool."

They showered, swam several laps, and flopped on lounge chairs that bordered the pool.

"How does it feel to be the First Lady?"

"One thing really bugs me," Jennie said. "See that guy over there? He or some other agent follows me everywhere. I can't get used to being watched constantly."

"It's for your own protection," Nikki said.

"I know but it still makes me nervous."

"Have you been doing anything as a First Lady yet?"

"No. I should attend some organizations and get involved."

"Sounds good."

"Would you help?"

"I'd love to," Nikki said. "Call me when you need me."

A short while later Jennie was back in the White House. She walked by her residence and knocked on another door.

Peter opened it and gaped at Jennie. "What a surprise. Please come in."

The agent followed her into the living room. Jennie pointed to another room and said to him, "You can sit in the den and watch television."

Peter and Jennie sat down across from each other. "I got rid of that agent so we can have some privacy."

Peter blushed. "Would you like something to eat or drink?"

"Ice tea with no sugar would be great."

A few minutes later the housekeeper served them tea.

Peter stared at Jennie. "Why have you got a running suit on?"

"I stopped here after exercising."

Peter sighed. "Peggy loved to go to the spa."

"I know," said Jennie. "I went with her many times."

Peter's eyes filled with tears. "I miss her, Jennie. I miss her a lot."

His body shook and tears flowed down his face. Jennie dashed to his side and embraced him. Suddenly, their lips met for a long, passionate kiss.

Peter broke away. "Sorry. I didn't mean to do that. Please forgive me."

Jennie's face was crimson. "I guess we both got carried away." She grabbed her coat. "I've got to go. Brenner's probably wondering where I am."

"Thanks for stopping," Peter said. "But you don't have to check up on me anymore. I'm doing better."

"What about dinner with us every other night?"

"We'll see. I'll let you know."

Jennie and the agent walked back to her place. She could still feel Peter's wet lips on hers and the thrills that engulfed her body. She yearned for more.

Jennie entered her residence and peeked in the den. She discovered Brenner staring into space with the television off.

"I'm back."

There was no response. She walked in front of him. "You look like you lost your best friend. What is wrong?"

Brenner shrugged his shoulders. "Just exhausted. How was the spa?"

"Great. It's fancier than the one I used to go to and the dues are less."

He glanced at this watch. "It's 11 o'clock. Kind of late for the spa, isn't it?"

"I stopped at Peter's for a few minutes."

Brenner's face reddened and his lips tightened. "I told you not to go there again. You never listen to me."

Jennie lowered her eyes. "That's the last time. He is improving every day so I don't have to stop there again."

"Will he still be coming to dinner?"

"I'm not sure."

"Enough of this talk." Jennie grabbed his hand. "Come get some sleep. You look terrible."

When they got into bed, Jennie kissed his cheek lightly and turned away. She lay awake for a long time thinking about Peter and what it would be like to make love to him.

Brenner also lay wide-eyed and filled with pain while he thought about confronting life without Bunny.

Chapter Twenty

The succeeding days were hectic for Brenner. He had to learn what the previous administration had accomplished and what needed to be done. He called Peter in his office for a review of his findings.

"We've got our work cut out for us."

"Yes," Peter said. "It will take time but we will do it."

Brenner pointed to some figures. "Look at this. Japan has been making a bigger profit from their export goods than we are from ours. Any ideas on how we can improve this?"

Peter pondered for a few minutes. "We have to find out what their people like and make products they will buy."

"Sounds good," Brenner said. "Someone will have to go to Japan and talk to government officials and the people."

"Want me to go?" Peter asked.

Brenner shook his head. "No. I'll go. You take care of things here."

"Anything special you want done while you're gone?" asked Peter.

Brenner handed him some papers. "Review these issues and write down your ideas. Also, keep working on the crime topic."

"Got you covered." Peter got up and left.

Brenner completed the details for his trip and headed home.

"You're home early," Jennie said. "Are you all right?

Brenner nodded and took off his coat. "I've got to get ready to go to Japan."

"Japan? Why on earth are you going there?"

"To make some money."

"How are you going to do that?"

"By getting better trade relations," said Brenner.

Jennie shook her head. "I guess you know what you are doing. Can I go? I've never been to Japan."

"Not this time."

She pouted. "How long are you going to be gone?"

"As long as it takes to get some answers."

"And I'll be alone again." Deep lines appeared on Jennie's forehead. "What am I supposed to do while you're gone?"

"Get involved with something, maybe with Corey Brown's wife, Nikki," Brenner said. "Find a project that will help others."

"What kind of project?"

"Read up on other wives of presidents and things they have done. That will give you some ideas."

"Can't wait."

Brenner sighed. "For now, could you help me pick out some clothes to wear on the trip?"

She followed him to their room and helped him pack.

"When do you leave?" Jennie asked.

"Six in the morning."

After a couple of long days alone, Jennie visited the library and came back with several books about the wives of former presidents. She skimmed them, took some notes, and made a phone call. "Nikki, could you meet me for lunch today?"

Jennie walked into a restaurant a couple of hours later and found Nikki in a back room.

"It feels great to get out," Jennie said.

"Have you heard from Brenner?" asked Nikki.

"He called when he got there."

"What have you been doing with yourself?"

"A lot of reading about other first ladies and how they occupied their time."

"Anything interesting?"

"The reading program fascinated me," Jennie said. "Would you like to help me with it?"

"What would we have to do?" asked Nikki.

"Read to kids and have them read to you."

Nikki thought for a moment. "Yes. I would like that. When do we start?"

"As soon as we set up a schedule." Jennie handed her a piece of paper. "Here is a list of schools in the area. Could you contact them for me with the idea?"

"I'll begin this afternoon."

"Wonderful." Jennie's eyes sparkled. "Working with kids will be fun. I can't wait to get started."

The phone woke Jennie. "Morning," she said with a big yawn.

"Sorry to call so early, but my schedule is tight," Brenner said. "I've got meetings all day."

Jennie looked at the clock...7 a.m. "No problem. How is everything going?"

"Great. I'm working on the best trade agreement our country has ever had with Japan."

"That's wonderful," said Jennie.

"What about you? Did you find a project to keep you busy?"

"Yes. Nikki and I are reading with school children. I love it. Kind of helps fill the void of not having our own kids."

There was silence for a few moments. "Glad you are keeping busy."

"When will you be home?"

"I'm not sure," said Brenner. "Whenever this trade agreement is signed. It should be settled in another week. I will let you know when I'm leaving."

"Good luck." Jennie hung up the phone and realized that it did not matter when Brenner got home.

Nikki and Jennie spent the next day in an elementary school. Jennie especially enjoyed working with the youngest children. While she read a picture book to them, a little girl sat at her feet wide-eyed and listened. The rest of the children swarmed around her and sat in a circle. Jennie finished the story with misty eyes and hugged each child before they went back to class.

"Thanks, Nikki, for helping. I love working with these children. What about you?"

Nikki nodded. "It's a wonderful experience. These kids are great."

After school Jennie stopped at the health center, worked out, and went home. She walked past her place and knocked on another door. Peter opened the door and gazed at her. "Come in."

"I stopped for a minute to see how you are doing." Jennie walked into the living room and instructed her bodyguard to go to the den.

"I'm doing better," said Peter. "What about you?"

"I am working on a reading program with school kids and love it."

"Good for you."

"And you?" Jennie asked. "Are you keeping busy?"

"I am too busy, doing the president's duties plus mine."

"That will keep you out of trouble." Jennie stood up. "Well, I have to go. You need your rest."

"Thanks for coming," Peter said.

All of a sudden Jennie threw her arms around his neck and gave him a long, fiery kiss. Peter responded with desire. Without a word, he took her hand, led her to his room, and bolted the door behind them. His gaze captured hers and their lips met with a longing passion. Jennie's head spun from the searing heat that traveled fast as lightning through her veins.

Peter picked her up and carried her to the bed. He knelt before her, unbuttoned her blouse, and unfastened the front hooks of her bra and cast it aside. While he massaged her soft breasts, his tongue lightly touched her bulging nipples and moved downward over her whole body.

The pleasure for Jennie was explosive.

She groaned and moaned. "Oh, Peter. Give it all to me. I am ready for you." Jennie pressed against his body.

Peter put his finger on her lips. "Sh-h-h-h. You don't want the bodyguards to hear us."

She nodded and pulled his head down for a wet, hot kiss. Peter's hands trembled as he slipped off her skirt and silk panties. He tore off his pants and entered Jennie's eager body. Her hands held on to his shoulders and dug into his muscular flesh while Jennie offered herself to Peter completely.

All the stars in the heavens seemed to explode at once as they climaxed together. They shuddered and embraced.

Jennie snuggled close to Peter. "Sex with you is more wonderful than I imagined. The best I've ever had."

Peter sat up and hung his head. "I'm ashamed of myself for letting this happen. You must not come back here again."

"Didn't I please you?"

"Too much. But we have to cool it," Peter said. "We can't take a chance of Brenner finding out."

"He will never know."

"It's too risky."

Jennie caressed his body. "Since I won't be back, how about making love one more time?"

Peter could not resist her beautiful, enticing body and they experienced ecstasy once more.

Jennie dressed and kissed him softly. "Are you sure you want me to stay away from you?"

"No, but you have to."

Jennie's eyes were misty as she dashed out the door.

Back in her room, she lay awake for hours, visualizing every movement that she and Peter made. Her body tingled all over with the memory of his touch. How would she be able to stay away from him?

Early the next morning Jennie rubbed her eyes and picked up the phone.

"Great news," Brenner said. "The agreement is signed."

Jennie yawned. "That means you will be home soon?"

"Tomorrow."

Her heart raced. "Good. See you then."

She hung up the phone and waited to feel excitement for the return of her husband, but the only thing she experienced was emptiness.

Jennie had breakfast, showered, dressed, and went to a middle school with Nikki.

On the way back, Jennie said, "I enjoyed working with the bigger kids almost as much as the little ones."

"They were cute, weren't they," said Nikki. "And so smart."

Jennie smiled. "They sure are. Hope we do this for a long time."

"Until they run out of kids," laughed Nikki.

"Just wish I could have one of my own," Jennie said.

"Have you tried lately?"

"Brenner wants to wait. He's always got an excuse."

"When the time is right, you will have a baby."

Jennie frowned. "The time will never be right."

"For now, you'll have to enjoy other people's kids."

"Looks that way." Jennie lowered her eyes.

"How about going to the spa after dinner?" asked Nikki.

"Sounds good."

They met at the health center that evening, did their aerobic exercises, and swam several laps in the pool.

"Glad you suggested this," Jennie said. "I should sleep good tonight."

Brenner greeted Jennie about two o'clock the following day. After a long hug he said, "It's great to be home."

"Good to see you," Jennie said.

They proceeded into the den where Brenner chatted endlessly about his trip. Jennie nodded and smiled.

Martha served them tea and cookies. "Sure is good to have you back, Mr. Sands. The place is too quiet without you."

"Thank you, Martha. I'm happy to be back."

"You're looking better than when you left," said Jennie. "You don't seem so depressed."

"It did me good to get away and achieve an important goal," Brenner said. "What about you? Tell me about your project."

"I love working with kids." Jennie edged closer to her husband. "Could we have one of our own? The campaign is over."

"We'll see. Maybe we can try soon."

"Do you mean it?"

"Of course."

She kissed his cheek. "Want to try now?"

"Not yet."

After dinner Brenner said in a low voice. "I took my pill. Want to see if it works?"

"Sure."

Dressed in a black teddy, Jennie lay in bed waiting for Brenner. Thoughts of making love to Peter entered her mind. She yearned to be with him. Brenner slid beside her. Jennie cringed when he kissed her and caressed her body. While he made love to her she realized that she wanted a baby, but she no longer wanted her husband.

While they lay quiet in each other's arms, Brenner seemed sexually satisfied, but Jennie felt unfulfilled and frustrated.

"What's wrong, Jennie? You used to beg me for sex. Tonight you laid there like a corpse."

"Nothing's wrong."

Brenner sat up and peered down at her. "Have you been seeing Peter again?"

"Of course not."

"I better not catch you near his place," Brenner said.

"No chance of that."

Chapter Twenty-One

Peter entered the president's office. "Did you hear about the trouble that has started again in Iraq?"

"Yes," Brenner said. "Looks like one of us will have to pay Saddam Hussein a visit."

"I'll go this time," Peter said.

"I would appreciate that. I should stay here with Jennie."

"Is something wrong?"

"I hope not. She's pregnant."

Peter gaped at him. "You're kidding!"

Brenner shook his head. "It has taken many years for her wish to come true. She is ecstatic."

"Are you happy about it?"

"I'm stunned."

Peter shook his hand. "Congratulations. The best of luck to both of you." His eyes were downcast. "I hope she does better than Peggy."

"That's why I'm so worried."

"You should not be too troubled about it," said Peter with a smile. "Jennie is a strong person. She'll do well."

"As long as she stays away from the booze," Brenner said. "I've instructed Martha to keep a close eye on her."

"That should ease your mind."

"A little."

"Not to change the subject," said Peter. "But can I ask you a question about my trip?"

"Of course. What is it?"

"Have you any ideas on how to tame Hussein?"

Brenner rested his head on his hands. After a couple of minutes he looked at Peter. "I think we should lift some sanctions."

"I'm not sure about that," said Peter. "How will he learn his lesson?"

"If we can show him that we can improve the care of his people, he may not be so aggressive," Brenner said.

"You may be right."

"To ensure your safety, I will give you extra protection."

"Thanks." Peter shook Brenner's hand and headed home to prepare for the trip.

Brenner took care of a few more matters and left. When he got home, he searched for Jennie.

"Martha!" he yelled.

She scampered into the room. "What is it, sir?"

"Where's Mrs. Sands?"

"At the spa."

"She's pregnant. What is she doing exercising?"

"Her doctor told her it is good for her."

"Dumb doctor." Brenner glared at Martha. "Why aren't you with her?"

"A security agent brought her there. I didn't think it was necessary for me to go too."

He pointed a finger at her. "From now on whenever my wife leaves this house with anyone, you go with them." Brenner frowned at her while his voice got louder. "Is that clear?"

Martha stared at the floor. "Yes, sir."

Brenner softened his voice. "Sorry, Martha. I didn't mean to yell at you. It's our first baby and I am nervous about it all."

"I understand, sir," Martha said. "Is there anything else?"

"That's it for now."

Martha went back to the kitchen to finish dinner.

An hour later Jennie walked through the door. Brenner rushed to her. "Thank God you're home. Are you all right?"

"Of course. Why wouldn't I be?"

"Martha told me you went to the spa. That's dangerous for a woman in your condition."

"No, it isn't. I talked to Dr. Wilkie and he approved of my going there. He said it was good for me."

"Never heard of such a thing."

"It's the modern way," Jennie said. "It will make the delivery easier."

Brenner lowered his eyes. "Or one like Peggy had."

"Nonsense. I feel great."

"That's what Peggy said."

"Call my doctor right now," said Jennie. "He will tell you that it is healthy to work out."

Brenner glanced at his watch. "It's 7 o'clock. He won't be there."

"Call him tomorrow."

"I will."

That night Jennie snuggled close to her husband. She whispered in his ear. "Did you take the pill?"

"Don't get any ideas. Do you want to hurt the baby?"

"I'm only three months pregnant."

"If we have sex, you may lose the baby."

"No way."

"You are the one who wanted a baby," Brenner said. "Now that you are pregnant, you want to take all these chances."

"I can't believe it. You're so paranoid." Jennie moved far away from him, relieved that he didn't want to make love to her.

Brenner called Dr. Wilkie the following morning. "Did you approve of Jennie going to the spa?"

"Yes," said the doctor. "A sensible exercise program, especially swimming, will help her during her pregnancy."

Brenner hesitated. "How's she doing?"

"She is as strong as a horse."

On the way home, Brenner stopped at Dr. Levin's for a physical and some tests. The doctor called him with the results two days later.

Brenner approached Jennie that evening with drooping shoulders and a paled face.

"What's wrong?" she asked. "You look like you've seen a ghost."

He glared at her while his bottom lip quivered. "Whose baby are you carrying?"

"Yours, of course. What are you implying?"

"You're lying."

"Have you gone mad?"

"I went to Dr. Levin the other day and he took some tests. He called me this afternoon with the results."

"What did he say?" asked Jennie.

"He confirmed what I had been told years ago, that I'm sterile."

"Dr. Levin must be mistaken. See another doctor for a second opinion."

Brenner grabbed her shoulders. "He's positive that I'm sterile. It's impossible for me to be a father. Now tell me, who have you been sleeping with?"

Jennie lowered her eyes. "I can't tell you."

He started to shake her. "Is it Peter? Is he the father?"

Tears filled Jennie's eyes. "No...no! Please, stop. You'll hurt the baby."

Brenner let go. "I'm moving into the spare bedroom. From this day forward, I will never touch you again, you slut!"

Jennie scampered into the bedroom, lay on the bed, and burst into tears. She ran her fingers gently over her tummy.

"I've got to be strong for you, baby. I've wanted you for so long."

Chapter Twenty-Two

Days passed without Jennie seeing her husband. He worked late every night and left early in the morning before she awakened.

One evening he knocked on Jennie's door. "May I come in?"

"Of course." She sat on the edge of a chair while he stared at her.

"Are you ready to tell me who the father is?"

Jennie shook her head and bit her bottom lip.

"Have you told anyone who it is?"

"No."

Brenner paced with his hands behind his back. "I'll make a bargain with you. Pretend that the baby is mine and I will make sure you have the best care."

"Sounds good."

"The sleeping arrangements remain the same," Brenner said. "But in public we will act like the perfect couple."

Jennie nodded and shrugged. Brenner glanced at his wife with an icy expression, turned away, and hurried back to his room.

Despite the uncomfortable distance between Brenner and Jennie, she was happy with the new life growing inside of her. After a warm shower she climbed into bed and read another chapter in the book, <u>Your First Child</u>.

Jennie drifted into a peaceful sleep while she visualized rocking her baby.

During breakfast one morning Jennie put her hand on her belly. "Martha! Martha!"

The housekeeper dashed into the dining room. "What is it, Mrs. Sands? Is something wrong?"

"Oh, no. Nothing is wrong. I just felt the baby move. Isn't that wonderful?"

Martha sighed. "Yes, ma'am, wonderful. You will be feeling lots of those."

"I hope so. Does that mean the baby is healthy?"

"Yes, ma'am."

Jennie grinned and rubbed her stomach gently. "I want this baby more than anything."

"I know, ma'am. And you'll be a terrific mother."

"Thanks, Martha."

Jennie finished her breakfast and took her morning walk with an agent close behind. Soft breezes flowed through her auburn hair and her cheeks glowed while she walked in a brisk manner, her arms swinging in rhythm to each step.

Brenner peered out of his office window and saw Jennie walk by. Peter had returned from Iraq and was ready to report the news to the president.

"That stupid woman," Brenner said.

"What woman?" Peter asked.

Brenner pointed out the window. "My wife. She is out there walking."

"Does she have someone guarding her?"

"Yes."

"Then what is the problem?"

"She is pregnant."

Peter shook his head. "Pregnant women can walk. What is wrong with that?"

"How can you say that after what happened to Peggy?"

"Peggy had complications and was weak. Jennie is strong."

Brenner walked back to his desk. "Forget it. Tell me about Iraq."

"You look worried," Peter said. "Is something wrong with Jennie?"

Brenner frowned. "No. Everything is fine. How was your trip?"

"Great. We dropped some of the sanctions. It helped our negotiations a great deal."

"Good. The next place to go is Russia. I need to check on their nuclear arms situation."

"You're going?"

"Yes."

"What about Jennie? You are going to leave when she is pregnant?"

"Martha will be with her."

"Want me to check up on her at times?"

"Thanks, if you don't mind."

Peter gave Brenner his report, and went back to his office.

A few days later Jennie answered the door. "Peter. You surprised me! Please come in."

She led him to the dining room. "Martha, set another place for dinner."

"Don't bother," Peter said. "I stopped to see how you are doing. I promised Brenner that I would check up on you."

"Please stay for dinner," said Jennie. "I'd love the company."

"O.K. Just this once."

Minutes later they were enjoying Martha's home cooking.

Peter stared at Jennie. "How are you feeling?"

"I never felt better."

"You are radiant. Carrying a baby agrees with you."

Jennie's eyes sparkled. "Thanks. It is the best thing that has ever happened to me." She stood up, turned sideways, and ran her hands over her tummy. "Does it show yet?"

Peter studied her for a moment and blushed. "A wee bit."

"I can't wait, Peter," Jennie said. "I am going to have a baby after years of waiting. Can you believe it?"

He smiled. "I'm very happy for you and Brenner. You are two lucky people."

Her eyes were down cast. "Yeah, lucky."

"What's wrong?"

"Nothing. I feel very lucky, but I am not so sure Brenner shares the same feeling."

"I think he is thrilled," Peter said. "What seems to bother him most is that you may hurt yourself."

Jennie appeared brighter. "Guess that is it."

"I must go," said Peter. "Take care of yourself and that baby."

"I will. Thanks for stopping by."

Peter kissed her lightly on the cheek and hurried out the door.

Jennie went to her room, played romantic music, and reminisced about being with Peter. Would she ever tell him the truth about the baby? Maybe some day, if the time was right.

For now, she would pretend that Brenner was the father.

Chapter Twenty-Three

Peter stopped by two or three times a week. Jennie looked forward to his visits, even though their relationship was platonic. He inquired about her health and encouraged her to take good care of her body.

During dinner one evening Jennie stared at Peter across the table. Their eyes met and her face turned crimson.

"Why are you looking at me that way?" Peter asked.

"Just thinking about the time you and I…"

"You and I what?"

"You know. The night we got together at your place."

Peter whispered, "Be careful. Martha may hear you."

Jennie spoke in soft tones. "It was beautiful. Wish we…"

"Stop wishing. It will never happen again."

"Don't say never, please."

"You're pregnant with Brenner's baby now," said Peter with tight lips and a shaky voice. "We can't talk about that incident ever again."

"I won't, but I will never forget it."

Peter got up and headed toward the door. "See you in a couple of days. Be careful and stay healthy."

He waved and left.

Jennie got a call from Peter a couple of days later.

"Brenner called," Peter said. "He'll be home tomorrow."

"Why didn't he call me?" asked Jennie.

"Guess he was too busy."

"Too busy to call me once? I haven't heard from him since he left."

"You'll have to ask him that."

Jennie hesitated. "Will you be stopping by for a visit tonight?"

"It won't be necessary. Your husband will be there soon."

"What about dinner some evening, just the three of us?"

"We'll see."

With trembling hands Jennie hung up the phone. She was not looking forward to Brenner's arrival.

She took a hot bath and dressed for a routine visit to her doctor.

After an examination, Dr. Wilkie checked her chart. "Weight is good and all vital signs are normal. The baby and you are doing well. How do you feel?"

"I feel fabulous. I can't wait for this baby to come."

"Are you interested in finding out if you are having a boy or a girl?"

"Not yet. Maybe in a month or two."

"Let me know when you are ready and I will make the arrangements."

"I will. Any instructions on keeping me healthy?"

"Keep up whatever you are doing. It is working," said Dr. Wilkie.

While Jennie walked to the car she felt some hard kicks. She touched her stomach and smiled. "You've got to be a boy because you move like a running back."

Jennie perceived that she was riding on a cloud all the way home.

Martha met her at the door. "Well, Mrs. Sands, what did the doctor say?"

"The baby and I are doing great."

"That's grand. Now you come over here and rest."

"I need exercise, not rest. I have to fetch my things. I'm going to the health center for a while."

"Lord have mercy. You can't exercise after all your running around."

"Martha, I only went to the doctor."

"He would not approve either."

"You're wrong. He told me to keep exercising."

"You know that Mr. Sands wouldn't like it and he'll be home tomorrow."

"Guess we won't tell him, will we?"

"I don't dare tell him. He will get very upset."

Jennie packed a tote bag and changed. Martha met her by the door.

"You don't have to go," said Jennie.

"Mr. Sands insisted that I go with you," Martha said.

"Oh, brother."

"You wouldn't let me go to the doctor's with you. But I have to go with you now or I'll get in trouble with Mr. Sands."

"O.K. Come on."

Inside the spa Martha said, "Do be careful, Mrs. Sands."

"Don't worry. I wouldn't do a thing to hurt this baby."

Jennie had cut down on her exercises and did the ones that were not too strenuous, most of them in the pool where the water soothed her body. The little one seemed to be trying to swim and appeared to like the water.

When they got home Martha said, "It's time to rest. You have been on the go all day."

Jennie hugged Martha and kissed her cheek. "Yes, ma'am. I am going to have a bite to eat then go to bed. How does that sound?"

Martha sighed. "Wonderful."

Jennie lay in bed with a relaxed body and mind. She was too exhausted to worry about how Brenner would react when he got home.

Right now, nothing else mattered but the baby growing bigger inside of her every day.

Chapter Twenty-Four

Brenner arrived home late in the afternoon.

Martha hurried to get his bags. "Welcome home, sir. How was your trip?"

"Could have been better. Where is Mrs. Sands?"

Martha headed briskly toward his room, carrying his suitcases. "Shopping, sir."

"What do you mean shopping?" He peered at his watch. "At three o'clock? She should be resting. And why aren't you with her?"

"She didn't tell me she was going."

"Then how do you know she is shopping?"

"I found this." She dug a piece of paper out of her apron pocket and handed it to him.

Brenner read the note that confirmed Martha's story and shook his head. "That woman never listens to anyone."

Suddenly the door burst open. Jennie entered the room carrying shopping bags in both hands.

"Brenner. You're home."

He glared at her. "Just in time to catch you gallivanting."

"I wasn't gallivanting. I did a little shopping."

Jennie walked up to him and kissed his cheek. "Come. I'll show you what I bought."

She grabbed his hand, led him into the den, and coaxed him to sit on the couch.

Jennie stood in front of him and pulled out each item. "Isn't this adorable?" She held up a white sleeper covered with pink and blue teddy bears.

Several items later she held up a baby's blanket. Brenner threw up his hands. "Enough already. All this junk looks the same to me."

Jennie put down the bag and pouted. "This is not junk. It's the start of the baby's wardrobe."

"I'm exhausted. Show me the rest another time."

She slumped into a chair. "You've got no interest in this baby, do you?"

"I'm taking care of the both of you. Isn't that enough?"

Jennie picked up her purchases and found Martha. Swooning and giggling could be heard from the kitchen. Brenner wished he could feel something besides the emptiness inside of him. He stretched out on the couch and closed his eyes.

A couple of hours later he felt a tug on his shoulder. "Get up. Dinner is ready," Jennie said.

Brenner sat up and rubbed his eyes. "I must have dozed off."

"Guess you were exhausted. Come, Martha has made your favorite dinner."

They sat down opposite each other and Martha served them two plates of steaming food.

Brenner's eyes twinkled. "How did you know I had a craving for this?"

Martha laughed. "Must have read your mind, sir."

He devoured the first helping and asked for seconds. "No one in the world makes chicken and dumplings like you, Martha." He licked his lips.

A huge smile covered her face while she placed a second helping in front of him.

"What about you, Mrs. Sands? Can I get you more?" asked Martha.

"No thanks. It's very good, but I've had enough."

"Don't forget. You're eating for two."

"I feel like I ate for three."

Jennie looked at Brenner. "You haven't said a word about your trip to Russia. How was it?"

"Not so good."

"Why do you say that?"

"There's a lot of unsettled business. It's going to take longer than I thought to get an agreement."

"What kind of unsettled business?" Jennie asked.

Brenner frowned. "I don't want to talk about it. Let's drop it."

"Fine."

They ate in silence for a while. "How do you feel?" asked Brenner.

"Dr. Wilkie said that we are both doing well."

"That's good news."

"He asked if I wanted to find out if I am having a boy or a girl. What do you think?"

Brenner shrugged. "Doesn't matter to me."

"Can't you give an opinion?"

"It's your baby," Brenner said.

"You said we would pretend it is yours."

Martha appeared behind Brenner with a crimson face and cleared the table. "Would either of you like tea?"

"None for me," Brenner said.

Jennie shook her head.

After Martha went back to the kitchen, Brenner said, "I wonder how much she heard."

"I'm not sure."

"Be careful what you say from now on."

"That goes for you, too."

They left the table and went to their separate bedrooms. Jennie lay all the baby clothes across the bed and gloated over each one. Four more months and her baby would be wearing them.

She felt a hard kick.

Chapter Twenty-Five

Brenner went through the motions of running the country, but his heart was no longer in it.

Peter was assuming more of the responsibilities every day. He confronted Brenner about the situation. "I'm swamped lately. Can you please do more?"

"I'll try, but I feel so damned depressed."

"Why? You're going to be a father. You should be elated."

"Yeah...elated."

His secretary called the president on the intercom. "Sir, there's a Detective Griffin here to see you. Should I show him in?"

Brenner hesitated. "Yes."

Peter got up to leave. "Stay," Brenner said. "I may need you."

The detective walked in behind the secretary and shook the hands of Brenner and Peter.

Once they were seated Brenner asked, "What can we do for you today?"

"I've learned that Bruce Rivers, Mike Ryan, and Raymond Masters visited Dr. Levin before they died."

"What does that prove?"

"They all died the next day," said Detective Griffin.

Deep lines penetrated Brenner's forehead. "It is a coincidence."

"Perhaps. Were you aware that they had all seen the doctor at those times?"

"No. They didn't check with me."

"What do you know about their deaths?"

"Only what I've told you many times," Brenner said. "The autopsies showed they all died from natural causes."

"I will have to check the autopsy reports."

"I think you're wasting your time," said Brenner.

Detective Griffin smiled. "If so, there is nothing for anyone to worry about, is there?"

"Right."

The detective stood up and shook Brenner's hand. "Thanks for your time. I'll contact you if I learn something."

"Please do."

After the detective left Brenner sighed. "I thought this was all over."

"Looks like it's just begun," Peter said.

"I'm going home," said Brenner. "I have to figure this out."

"I'll cover for you."

"Thanks."

Brenner got home and poured himself a glass of straight whiskey.

Jennie walked into the den. "You're home early. Anything wrong?"

He gulped down the whiskey. "Detective Griffin paid me a visit today."

"Is that why you took that drink?"

"Yes. I needed to unwind."

"Why? What did he say?"

"Seems like he is still investigating the deaths of Bruce and the others."

"I thought those cases were closed."

"So did I."

"Don't let it trouble you," said Jennie. "We both know there is nothing to find."

"You're right," said Brenner as he forced a smile. "If you don't mind, I'm going to my room for a while. I am exhausted."

He lay on his bed and fell into a deep sleep. Bruce Rivers appeared in his dreams His distorted face moved closer to Brenner.

"Help me…help me," cried Bruce.

His face and body started to drip blood. In seconds he melted into a pool of blood at Brenner's feet. Brenner tried to run from the scene, but his feet were frozen in place. He screamed on the top of his lungs.

Jennie rushed into the room and shook him. "Brenner. Wake up."

He jumped up and trembled. "It was only a dream. Thank God."

"It must have been a nightmare from the way you were yelling."

"That bad?"

"They must have heard you in New York," Jennie said.

"Sorry."

"Want to tell me about it?" asked Jennie.

"No. I don't want to relive it."

Jennie took his hand. "Come with me and have a cup of coffee. The whiskey must have given you bad dreams."

Brenner nodded. "That must be it."

Later that evening Brenner got a phone call.

"Anything wrong?" Brenner asked.

"Hope not," said Dr. Levin. "Joe Griffin is stopping by my office tomorrow. Do you know anything about it?"

"He came to my office today. Sounds like he is still snooping."

"What did he say?"

"He wants to see your autopsy reports," Brenner said.

"What the hell for?"

"He found out that Mike and the rest were at your office the night before they died."

"How did he find out? You tell him?" asked Dr. Levin.

"No, I didn't tell him. I have no idea who did."

"Damn. This could mean trouble. What should I tell him?"

"Nothing," said Brenner. "And make sure those autopsies don't reveal anything."

"I am sure they don't."

Brenner lay on his bed and tried to sort out the latest events surrounding the deaths of Bruce and the other politicians. He hoped everything would be settled soon. He closed his eyes and dozed off.

Mike Ryan appeared before him with blood dripping from his mouth and hands.

"Save me. Please help me," he cried out. He walked close to Brenner then dissolved into a pool of blood.

Brenner's feet were covered with blood. He attempted to scream, but no sounds would come out.

His eyes slowly opened.

Brenner peeked around the room for Mike and discovered that he was alone. He breathed a sigh of relief when he realized that the bad scenes had disappeared. Sweat poured down his face while his hands shook.

He wondered how long these nightmares would continue.

Dr. Levin called him the following evening.

"How did it go?" asked Brenner.

"I don't like this one bit," Dr. Levin said. "Detective Griffin said they may exhume the bodies."

"What the hell for?"

"To see if they did die from natural causes." His voice escalated. "What if they find something?"

"After all this time, is it possible?" asked Brenner.

"Yes, and if they do find something, I'm not taking the full blame for you."

"Calm down. There's no reason to panic."

"Hope you're right."

Brenner took a deep breath. "What else did he say?"

"He wanted copies of the autopsies."

"Did you give them to him?"

"I couldn't. They are at my house. I'll get them to him soon."

"That shouldn't be a problem if they were prepared carefully. Anything else happen?"

Dr. Levin sighed. "Amber, my fiancee, heard the whole thing and decided to explore on her own."

"What did she do?"

"I caught her going through my files at home. She looked scared when I walked in."

"What did you tell her?"

"Nothing, but I think she knows too much."

"Why do you say that?"

"Like the others, she is getting nosey about your former secret lover," Dr. Levin said. "What scares me more is that she may know my part in all of this."

"How are you going to handle it?"

"I'm not sure. I have to think about it."

"Maybe she can be sworn to secrecy," Brenner said.

"Perhaps."

"Be careful what you say and do from now on, including telephone calls."

"I will," said Dr. Levin. "Tomorrow I am taking a day off and going to the beach with Amber. I've got to try to relax."

"Sounds good. Keep in touch."

The phone clicked in Brenner's ear. He felt like everything was closing in on him.

Jennie walked into the den. "You are trembling. Are you all right?"

"I just feel a little chilled. Think I'll go to bed." He kissed her cheek and went to his room. After a hot shower he climbed into bed.

Brenner lay awake for hours with thoughts about the latest happenings in his life, and finally dozed off. In his dreams he was walking in the middle of a cemetery. All of a sudden three graves opened up at once. Bruce Rivers, Mike Ryan, and Raymond Masters emerged and leaped toward Brenner.

"Murderer," they yelled while they chased him around the cemetery and jumped on him. Brenner gasped, breathless, then felt his body sinking lower, and faster, into a gigantic hole.

Jennie ran to his side and tugged his arm. "Wake up!"

Brenner opened his eyes and glanced around the room. He buried his face in his clammy cold hands while his body shook from head to toe.

"I can't take any more of this."

"You were breathing hard and whimpering," said Jennie. "Did you have another nightmare?"

Brenner grimaced. "Three in the past two days."

"What are they about?"

"I can't tell you."

"Perhaps Dr. Levin can help," Jennie said. "Maybe he can give you sleeping pills."

"Then they would get me for sure."

"What are you talking about? Who will get you?"

Brenner shook his head. "I can't say. Hear me? I just can't say."

Jennie threw her arms up in the air. "I can't help you if you won't tell me what is happening with you."

Brenner's voice escalated. "Don't you understand? You can't help me. Nobody can. I am doomed."

"You are acting crazy. Either you call Dr. Levin and get some help, or I will."

Brenner let out a deep sigh. "I'll call him tomorrow."

"Good," said Jennie. "Are you going to be all right now?"

"Yeah. I think so."

Jennie kissed his forehead. "Get some sleep." She viewed him with concern and quietly left the room.

Brenner could not fall back to sleep because he feared the dead men would appear again. He got up and tiptoed into the kitchen to fix some hot tea.

A shaky voice could be heard in the dark. "Is someone there?"

Brenner's heart pounded. "Who is it?"

A light flashed on. "Just me. What are you doing in the dark?"

"Martha, you startled me."

"Sorry, but you scared me too. I thought you were a burglar." Martha studied Brenner. "Are you all right, Mr. Sands. You don't look so good."

"I am having some trouble sleeping. I was about to make a cup of hot tea to help me sleep."

"Wait a minute," said Martha. "I'll prepare you my remedy."

Brenner watched her put some milk in a pan.

In minutes she handed him a cup of warm milk. "This will help you sleep better than tea. It works every time."

"Thanks."

"I'm going back to bed," Martha said. "You should be able to sleep now, sir."

"Hope so."

Brenner finished his milk and returned to his bed. After staring at the ceiling for an hour, he picked up a book and read most of the night. Every time his eyes started to close, he jumped and opened them wide. He dreaded another encounter with those bloody ghosts.

Peter stopped in Brenner's office the next day. "You look terrible. What happened?"

"I couldn't sleep last night."

"Because of the investigation?" Peter asked.

"No. Because of my nightmares."

"What kind of nightmares?"

"They are horrible. I can't talk about them."

"Call Dr. Levin today," said Peter.

Brenner scowled. "He's gone to the beach for the day."

"Try him later."

"I've got to see him soon," Brenner said. "I feel like I am going crazy."

"It's your nerves. I am sure the doctor can help you."

Brenner was wide-eyed while his hands trembled. "He's got to. I can't stand it any more."

There was no escape for Brenner. After Peter left a face with bulging eyes appeared on the wall…Bruce's.

Chapter Twenty-Six

Brenner found Detective Griffin seated in front of his office when he arrived for work.

He smiled at him while his heart raced. "What brings you here so early?"

"Can we go inside and talk?" asked the detective.

Once they were seated Brenner asked, "What's up?"

"Amber Green's dead."

Brenner was sullen. "Oh, God. How?"

"She apparently drowned."

"What do you mean apparently? Aren't you sure of the cause of death?" asked Brenner.

"No. We'll know more after the autopsy."

"Is Dr. Levin doing it?"

"He and another doctor," said Detective Griffin. "I want a second opinion this time."

"I can't believe it. Dr. Levin must be upset."

"Actually, he is taking it quite well."

Brenner lowered his eyes. "He is probably in shock."

Detective Griffin stood up. "Perhaps." He walked toward the door and stopped. "I'll call you when the results of the autopsy are in."

After the detective left Brenner slipped out of the office and found a pay phone.

"Claude, what the hell happened?"

"Amber drowned."

"I know. Detective Griffin was just here," said Brenner. "She was a terrific swimmer. What went wrong?"

"She got too nosey."

"Damn! Detective Griffin is getting a second opinion on her death. Is there a chance that he will discover anything suspicious?"

"Don't worry," said Dr. Levin. "Everything's under control."

"Hope you're right."

Brenner went back to his office, stared into space, and wondered what else could go wrong.

Suddenly a figure appeared before him. Brenner blinked several times but it became more visible and moved closer to him. He recognized the face, Raymond Masters. He moved up to Brenner's desk and laughed. Brenner reached out to touch him but the figure disappeared. Laugher was heard behind his desk. Brenner turned and saw Raymond. He got up, raced into Peter's office, and collapsed into a chair with his face in his hands.

"What's wrong?" asked Peter. "You look like you have seen a ghost."

Brenner peered through his fingers while his eyes circled the room. "Did anyone follow me in here?"

"No. Who did you expect?"

"Raymond."

"Nonsense. Raymond is dead."

"He was in my office, laughing at me." Brenner peeked through his fingers behind him. "Sure he didn't follow me?"

Peter shook his head. "You're losing it."

"I can't stand it anymore," Brenner said. "They are all after me."

"Who's after you?"

"Bruce...Mike...Raymond."

"They are all dead. How could they get you?"

Brenner's hands shook. "First in my dreams, and lately, during my waking hours. I can't escape them."

"Take your hands off your face and look at me," Peter said.

Brenner dropped his hands in his lap and clasped them until they turned red. He lifted his eyes slowly and stared at Peter.

"You've got to help me. I'm going out of my mind."

"I can see that," Peter said. "Have you been sleeping at all?"

"No. I'm afraid they will come."

"You do need help, but I'm no doctor. Call Dr. Levin. Maybe he can give you some medication to make you sleep."

"He'll probably give me pills so I won't wake up."

Peter frowned. "Why do you say that?"

Brenner leaned forward and talked in low tones. "What about the others, and now Amber?"

"What happened to Amber?"

"She drowned yesterday."

"Oh, my God!" Peter said. "What the hell happened? She was a very good swimmer."

"I know. That's why I don't think it was an accident," Brenner said. "An autopsy should reveal the truth."

"An autopsy for a drowning?" Peter asked.

"To make sure there was no foul play, I guess."

"Who's giving it?"

"Dr. Levin and another doctor assigned by Detective Griffin."

"Oh, no. More meetings with our favorite detective."

"We can't get away from him," Brenner said. "But with all that's happened, do you see why I don't want to go to Dr. Levin?"

"Not really. He wouldn't do anything to hurt you. He's your friend."

Brenner bit his bottom lip. "I don't have any friends. Who can I really trust?"

"I'm your friend and I care what happens to you." Peter put his arm around Brenner. "That's why I'm advising you to get to a doctor today."

"Not Dr. Levin. I'm afraid to go to him."

Peter grabbed a phone book and started flipping pages. His fingers ran down a page and stopped.

"What about Dr. Rango? He's a psychiatrist, and according to a friend of mine, a very good one. I'll make an appointment for you right now. Do you agree?"

Brenner pondered for a few moments. "O.K. But I am not telling him about Bruce and the others."

"Tell him what you want, but it is important to talk with him about your not sleeping. You can say you are having nightmares, with monsters. Just don't mention any names."

"O.K. I'll call him."

That afternoon Brenner was sitting across from Dr. Rango.

"How long have you had trouble sleeping?" asked the doctor.

"Three or four months."

"What is foremost on your mind?"

"I feel that I am a failure as president," Brenner said.

"How so?"

"I haven't fulfilled one campaign promise so far."

Dr. Rango peered at him over his gold-rimmed glasses. "Do you know why?"

Brenner sighed. "Congress votes against every proposal I make. My hands are tied."

"Have you analyzed why they do this?" the doctor asked.

"I'm the first independent to be voted president. Congress does not want me to succeed," said Brenner. "This country always has been a two party system. I am an outsider and that is the way they treat me. I am powerless."

"The articles I read show the people are behind you."

"According to the polls, congress ranks higher in popularity than I do," Brenner said. "I am slipping fast."

"How does that make you feel?"

"Frustrated. I was wrong to run as an independent. I think I would have a better chance getting some of my reformed programs approved as a republican or a democrat."

"I am not a politician so I can't help you there. But maybe the vice president or some members of congress you can trust can suggest a way to work with congress," Dr. Rango said.

"Sounds good. I'll talk with them."

The doctor wrote down some notes. "Is there anything else you want to talk about?"

"I've had a lot of nightmares lately," Brenner said.

"Describe them for me."

"Monsters chase me and try to kill me."

The doctor stared at him. "I read in the newspaper that you have had a lot of your friends die recently, right?"

"Yes."

"Maybe their loss is causing bad dreams."

"Could be."

"Something else may be bothering you more." The doctor tapped a pencil on his desk then gazed at Brenner. "Are you afraid that you will be next to die?"

"At times."

"Those thoughts could be causing your nightmares."

"Perhaps."

Dr. Rango scribbled a prescription and handed it to Brenner. "Here's something that should help you sleep. Take two pills three times a day. If they don't help, call me."

Brenner stood up. "I hope they work. I am a walking zombie."

"Come back a week from today and let me know how you are doing."

"Thanks, Doc."

Brenner got home about an hour later. Jennie greeted him with a kiss on the cheek. "You're home early."

"I had to see a doctor."

"I saw my doctor today, too." Jennie smiled. "We should have gone together."

"Not possible. I went to a shrink."

"A shrink? What for?"

Brenner pulled out some pills. "To help me sleep."

"I hope they work. I've been worried about you."

They walked into the den and sat on comfortable chairs.

Jennie frowned. "I read about Amber in the paper. Dr. Levin must be devastated."

"It was a terrible shock."

"When is the funeral?"

"Day after tomorrow."

"I want to go," said Jennie.

"No. It's not a good place to be when you're pregnant. I will go for both of us."

"If you insist."

Brenner sighed. "Let's talk about happier things. What did your doctor say?"

"The baby and I are doing great."

"That's wonderful. Glad to hear it."

"You do seem concerned about me and the baby. Am I right?"

Brenner nodded. "I wish the best for the both of you." A few tears fell softly on his cheeks. "After all, you are my friend, Jennie, aren't you?"

"Of course. Why do you ask that?"

He shrugged. "Just wondering."

Jennie smiled. "I'll be your best friend if you want."

More tears fell on his cheeks. "I would love that."

"I don't remember ever seeing you so emotional." Jennie walked over to him and put her arms around his shoulders. "Everything is going to be all right, Brenner. Once you take your medication and get some sleep, you will feel like a new person."

"Yes...sleep...got to get some sleep."

Martha put her head in the door. "Dinner is ready."

After they ate Brenner took two pills and went to bed. It was 7 p.m. when he fell into a deep sleep. Two hours later a figure with dark flowing hair, dressed in white, entered his dreams. Amber's beautiful face came into view. She beckoned him to follow her so she could show him something. Brenner ran in the opposite direction, yelling.

He woke up to Jennie shaking him. "Didn't you take your pills?"

"Yes."

"More nightmares?"

"Damn it, yes."

"Maybe it will take a couple of days to take effect."

Brenner pounded his pillow. "Or, maybe never." His whole body shook. "I don't know what to do, Jennie. These dreams are driving me crazy."

Jennie lay beside Brenner and held his head on her chest while she rocked him back and forth. "You're going to be fine. The pills have to work into your body. You will see the difference in a couple of days."

"They've got to. If they don't work I'll have to kill myself."

"Hush. You don't mean that. You'll feel great in a few days."

"Hope so." Brenner's head jerked. "Hey. I felt the baby kick, and what a kick."

Jennie laughed. "This baby is a cross between an acrobat and a football player."

"There's another one," Brenner said. "I would say a football player, and a very healthy one."

"Very active also."

Brenner sat up and gazed at Jennie. "I've got to get better to witness the baby being born."

"You mean you'd help in the delivery room?"

"I didn't mean that. I don't think I could actually watch a baby being born."

"Sure you could," said Jennie. "We are best friends, right?"

"Yeah, best friends." Brenner pondered for a few moments. "All right. I will go into the delivery room with you, but I'll probably faint."

Jennie squealed and threw her arms around his neck. "Thank you, Brenner. You've made me so happy."

"Calm down. You're hurting my neck." Brenner took her hands and put them by her sides.

Jennie whispered in his ear. "Couldn't we make a little love? It's been so long."

He turned crimson. "I am in no shape for that."

"Maybe after you catch up on sleep."

"Maybe when you tell me who the father of the baby is."

"Looks like we'll have to wait a while," Jennie said.

The phone rang and Brenner answered it. "Detective Griffin. What can I do for you?"

"Amber's autopsy came back."

"What are the results?"

"She was poisoned."

"It can't be. She drowned."

"Looks like she was poisoned first," the detective said. "Traces of cyanide were found in her blood."

"What happens now?" asked Brenner.

"We'll have to find the one who did it."

"Any suspects?"

"I don't want to mention names yet, but we do have at least one suspect," said the detective. "When we have enough evidence, we will make an arrest."

Brenner took a deep breath. "Is that it?"

"We're exhuming the bodies of Bruce and the others tomorrow."

"You're wasting your time. There is no connection between all of them."

"That is yet to be proven."

"Whatever."

"Goodnight and pleasant dreams," said Detective Griffin.

Brenner sat on the edge of the bed and shook his head.

"What is it?" asked Jennie. "Did someone else die?"

"Amber Green was poisoned."

"That can't be. The paper said that she drowned."

"Detective Griffin said that they found some cyanide in her blood."

"How terrible! Who would do such a thing?"

"I have no idea."

The phone rang and Brenner picked it up. "I heard about it. Who did this?"

"Are you accusing me?" Dr. Levin asked.

"Of course not."

"But that damn detective must suspect me. He questioned me for an hour."

"Weren't you the last one to see her?"

"There you go, accusing me again," said the doctor.

"No, I'm not. But maybe that's why the detective is questioning you."

"He knows nothing and neither do you," yelled Dr. Levin.

"Calm down."

"Easy for you to say," the doctor said. "What about those bodies they are digging up? Did you know about that?"

"Yes."

"What are we going to do if they find something?"

"I'm not sure. We'll have to get together and talk about it."

"Fine. I'll meet you in your office at nine in the morning," Dr. Levin said. "And you'd better have some good answers."

The phone banged in Brenner's ear.

"Who was that?" asked Jennie.

"Dr. Levin."

"How is he taking Amber's death?"

"Not too good."

"Is that why he is calling here so late?"

"Yeah."

Dr. Levin was waiting for Brenner when he arrived. They walked into the office with the secret service agents behind them. Brenner motioned to the agents to wait in another room.

Dr. Levin's hands trembled as he pointed a finger at Brenner. "Listen to me. I'm not taking the blame for any of this."

"I don't know what you are talking about."

"You know damn well what I am talking about, what they will find when they dig up the bodies."

"What is there to find?"

The doctor stood up and grabbed a tall heavy bookend and held it high in the air. "Will this help you remember?" He dashed toward him.

Brenner jumped out of his chair and yelled. "Stop it, you fool."

The agents hurried from the nearby room and witnessed commotion. Two shots were fired. The bookend crashed to the floor with a loud thump, inches away from the president. Dr. Levin slumped to the floor and lay motionless at Brenner's feet.

Brenner stared at the agents. "Why did you do that?"

"He was going to kill you, sir."

"No! No! Claude would not do that to me." He stumbled into his chair, lay his head down, and wept.

Chapter Twenty-Seven

Jennie walked up to Brenner who was seated in front of a window.

"Hi, Brenner. Look who came to visit you." She held a baby in front of him. "Isn't he adorable?"

Brenner's eyes did not blink.

"Chad Ashley Sands. Do you like it?"

He stared straight ahead.

Jennie continued to talk at a faster pace. "Chad is a week old today." She moved him closer to his face. "Look how long he is, twenty-one inches. And he weighs nine pounds already. Can you believe it?"

Jennie backed away when she got no reaction. "Maybe next time we visit you will know us."

She looked around the room at the other patients. Some watched television in a trance, others laughed to themselves. She shuddered and walked up to a nurse.

"Could I see Dr. Pierce, please?"

Jennie sat in the doctor's office a few minutes later.

"What a beautiful baby," Dr. Pierce said. "How did Mr. Sands react to him?"

"He didn't recognize us. It was scary. What's happening to him?"

"He has withdrawn from reality."

"Could the death of his friend, Dr. Levin, be causing this?" Jennie asked.

"I suspect that is the main reason."

Chad started to fuss a little. Jennie rocked him in her arms and kissed his cheek. She looked up at the doctor and said, "Brenner was having terrible nightmares a couple of months before coming in here. Does he still have them?"

"Yes and they seem more frequent the last couple of weeks. He wakes up screaming."

"That's what he did at home. He would never tell me what they were about. Did he tell you?"

"No. He never talks. But I have assigned an aide to stay in his room all night. He has heard him call out some names."

"What names?"

Dr. Pierce grabbed Brenner's chart. "Bruce, Raymond, Mike, Claude, and Bunny. He repeats at least one of the names before he screams."

"Those are the politicians that died and his doctor." Jennie shook her head. "Did you say, Bunny? Who on earth is she?"

"I have no idea," said Dr. Pierce.

"Why is he having nightmares about all of them?"

"I'm not sure, but he seems to get worse after Detective Griffin questions him."

"How does he react to him?"

"Nothing. Absolutely no response."

Jennie stared at Dr. Pierce. "How long will Brenner have to stay in this mental ward?"

"If his condition doesn't change, a long time."

Jennie got up and forced a smile. "Thanks for your time. I hope my husband is better when I visit again."

Martha greeted Jennie when she returned home. She took the baby and held him to her chest.

"Did you see your daddy, precious one?" She kissed him lightly on the cheek and looked at Jennie. "How is Mr. Sands, ma'am?"

"Not good, Martha. Not good at all."

"What did he say when he saw Chad?"

"He didn't recognize us. Can you believe that?"

"How terrible."

Jennie reached for Chad.

"You get freshened up, I'll take care of this little one," Martha said. "I've got dinner ready any time you want to eat."

Jennie took a hot shower, changed into a comfortable leisure outfit and joined Martha in the kitchen.

"Are you going to eat now?" Martha asked.

"I have to feed Chad first."

"I took care of him, ma'am. He's fed and dry."

"You are wonderful. I don't know what I would do without you."

"I hope you never have to do without me," Martha said. "I am very happy here with you, Chad, and Mr. Sands. I sure hope he gets home soon."

"We all need him home. Right, baby?" Jennie touched Chad's cheek gently. "Look, Martha, he smiled at me."

"Just gas, ma'am."

"You call it gas, I say it was a smile."

After Jennie finished her dinner the doorbell rang. Martha walked briskly to answer it. "Mr. Johnston. Come in, please."

He walked into the dining room. "Hi, Jennie. I stopped by to see how Brenner is doing." He peeked at Chad who was sleeping in Jennie's arms. "He looks content."

"Oh, yes. He is such a good baby." Her eyes sparkled. "I am a very lucky woman."

"Yes you are," Peter said.

"I wish Brenner could see him."

"Didn't you see him today?"

Her eyes lowered. "Yes, but he didn't recognize us. He is in another world."

Peter shook his head. "That's too bad. Did you talk to his doctor?"

She nodded. "He told me that Brenner could be like this for a long time."

"Doctors have been wrong."

"I hope this one is," Jennie said. "What about you? How are you handling all the affairs of the country?"

"I'm putting in some long hours but I am making it." He got up to leave. "I will stop by whenever I can to make sure you two are all right. Do you mind?"

"Not at all. I look forward to your visits."

Peter kissed Chad on the forehead. "Bye, little one."

He gave Jennie a peck on the cheek, waved to Martha, and dashed out the door.

"What a fine man," Martha said. "He is so busy yet he finds time to check on you."

Jennie smiled. "I agree. He is a true friend."

Martha approached her. "Let me help you with the baby."

"Thanks, but I will take care of him." Her eyes were misty as she held Chad close to her. "He is all I've got."

Chapter Twenty-Eight

Jennie picked up the phone. "Dr. Pierce. You surprised me. I was just going to leave for the hospital." She paused. "I hope you are calling to tell me that Brenner is better."

"Sorry. I can't tell you that because…Brenner is dead."

Jennie gasped. "No. It can't be." Her voice escalated. "How did it happen?"

"He hung himself."

"Oh, my God!" yelled Jennie as she hung up the phone.

Martha hurried into the den. "What's wrong, ma'am? You are as white as a ghost."

Jennie held her forehead and swayed back and forth. "I don't believe it."

"Sit down, Mrs. Sands, before you fall down." Martha took her arm and guided her into a chair. "Now, tell me what happened."

Jennie took a deep breath. "Brenner's dead."

"Mr. Sands, dead? No. It can't be."

Jennie's body trembled. "It's true. His doctor just called."

"How did he die?"

Jennie lowered her head. "I'm not quite sure. I've got to go to the hospital and find out the details."

Jennie looked around the room and scowled. "Where's Chad?"

"In the kitchen. I was feeding him when I heard you yell."

"Bring him in here at once."

"Yes, ma'am."

Martha scurried out of the room and returned in minutes.

"Give him to me," Jennie said. She embraced her son and cried. "I won't let anything happen to you."

Peter showed up a short time later in a limousine and two secret service agents who drove him and Jennie to the hospital.

She looked at Peter and started to cry. He put his arm around her and tried to comfort her.

Jennie lay her head on his shoulder. "Thanks for coming. I could not do this alone."

"You know I am always here for you."

She nodded and clung to Peter the rest of the way.

Ten minutes later they were seated across from Dr. Pierce.

"How could Brenner hang himself in a hospital?" Jennie asked. "And you said he was being watched around the clock."

"With bed sheets," the doctor said. "It happened when the aide stepped out of the room for a short period of time."

She shook her head. "When I saw him two days ago, he seemed too spaced out to do that."

"Something in his mind could have told him to do it."

Jennie turned to Peter. "Is it possible for Brenner to do that?"

He shrugged his shoulders. "The doctor knows more that I do."

"I suppose so." Jennie looked at Dr. Pierce. "We will have to start making funeral arrangements."

"Not until Detective Griffin has an autopsy performed."

"What for? It was a suicide."

"He wants to make sure."

"Whatever." She looked at the doctor. "Can I see Brenner now?"

"He's at the morgue."

Detective Griffin was standing over Brenner's body when Jennie and Peter walked in.

Jennie trembled while she peered at Brenner. "Why did you do this?"

Tears flowed down her cheeks.

Peter put his arm around her and stared at the motionless body. "I can't believe you killed yourself." His body shook and tears rolled down his cheeks.

He glanced at the detective. "Are you sure someone else didn't do it?"

Detective Griffin ran his fingers over the marks on Brenner's neck. "What shape do you see?"

Peter shrugged his shoulders. "Sort of a "V"."

"An inverted "V", the detective said.

"What does that prove?"

"The marks show he hung himself. If he was strangled by someone else, the bruise on the neck would have been a straight line caused by force from behind."

"Never heard of that," Peter said. "Then why are you having an autopsy taken?"

"To make sure he wasn't taking any hallucinating drugs to cause him to kill himself."

"Are you accusing Dr. Pierce of giving him harmful drugs on purpose?" Jennie asked.

"No. I'm just doing my job, ma'am."

"When is your job going to be done so I can make funeral arrangements?" asked Jennie.

"I will call you when we are finished. It shouldn't take more than a couple of days."

Jennie peeked at Brenner once more, closed her eyes, and shuddered. "Let's go, Peter, please."

They rode home in silence. Peter stopped at Jennie's door and said, "Don't hesitate to call me anytime, any hour."

"You're always there for me. How can I ever repay you for your support?"

He lifted her chin and gazed into her eyes. "You were there for me when Peggy died, remember?" He brushed his lips across her cheeks and hurried down the hallway.

Martha greeted Jennie as soon as she stepped inside. "Come rest, Mrs. Sands. I have hot tea waiting for you."

Jennie followed her into the kitchen. "Thanks, Martha. That would taste good about now." She leaned over the bassinet and stared at Chad sleeping peacefully on his back. "Has he been good?"

"An angel, as usual. He is a pleasure to take care of." Martha frowned. "It must have been a terrible night for you. Do you want to talk about it?"

"Not really. It has been a draining experience."

"I understand. But if you need me, I am here."

Jennie nodded, finished her tea, and picked up Chad. She pressed his little body next to hers and went to her room.

She lay in bed and gazed at the small figure in the crib. "You're going to need a daddy. When do I tell him about you?"

Chapter Twenty-Nine

Light snow mixed with sleet fell on the limousine that carried the president's body slowly down the road. Curious spectators lined up for miles to observe Brenner being taken to his final resting place. All of congress and the administration, Brenner's and Jennie's families, and the remaining members of Aces High were gathered at the gravesite.

The snow and sleet intensified while gusty winds stung their faces. After the minister finished his prayers, everyone quickly got into their vehicles and gathered together at Jennie's place.

Martha had food and drinks prepared for everyone.

Brenner's mother sat across from Jennie. "How are you doing, my dear?"

"Kind of numb from it all."

"It is difficult, especially being left alone with a baby. Maybe Chad will follow in his father's footsteps," Mrs. Sands said. "Did you know Brenner wanted to be president since he was eight years old?"

"No, he never told me," said Jennie. "But his dream did come true."

"For a while anyway." Brenner's mother's eyes filled with tears.

In another part of the room the former members of the Aces High Club were seated together.

"There are only four of us left," Corey said.

"Weird, isn't it?" said Chuck.

"Interested in recruiting some new members and starting again?" asked Rick.

"No way," Peter said.

"The poker club has brought us nothing but bad luck," Chuck said.

"We could change the name," said Rick.

They replied in unison, "No!"

Rick shrugged his shoulders and walked toward the long table of food.

Within an hour everyone had gone except Peter. He approached Jennie. "Are you going to be all right?"

"I hope so."

"I'm not far away if you need me."

"Thanks."

Peter kissed her cheek and went back to his place.

Jennie sat in Brenner's chair in the den and listened to some of his favorite music.

"Why, why did you kill yourself?" Tears fell softly on her cheeks as she reminisced about some of the good times they shared.

A couple of days later Peter stopped by. "Set another plate, Martha," Jennie said.

"Don't bother. I will only be a few minutes."

"Please stay. I hate eating alone."

"All right. If you insist."

Jennie studied his face. "You look worried. Is something wrong?"

Peter nodded. "Detective Griffin paid me a visit today."

"About Brenner's autopsy?"

"That was part of it."

"What were the results?"

"There were no hallucinating drugs in his body. His mind must have told him to kill himself."

"Then why are you worried?"

"The detective told me the findings of the bodies that were exhumed."

"And?"

"Cyanide was found in all of them."

"What does that prove?"

Peter spoke in low tones. "They were all murdered."

Jennie gasped. "How could that be? Why would anyone kill them?"

Peter frowned. "The detective examined Dr. Levin's records. Bruce, Mike, and Raymond were seen by him before they died."

"He thinks Dr. Levin poisoned them?"

"Yes."

Jennie put her hand to her mouth. "Oh, my God."

"What is it?"

"Brenner suspected something. "That's why he wouldn't go to Dr. Levin for help with his nightmares."

"Could be, but Detective Griffin feels Brenner may have had something to do with the murders."

"That's crazy."

"Telephone logs show that Brenner and Dr. Levin called each other before and after the murders."

"So?"

"They could have planned them together."

"Nonsense," Jennie said. "Brenner wasn't capable of killing anyone."

"I agree, but the detective thinks it was possible, or he could have arranged to have them killed," said Peter. "He also talked to Dr. Pierce and Dr. Rango about Brenner's nightmares. They both said that they could have occurred from guilt because of the killings."

"Why would he want them dead?"

Peter frowned. "That remains a mystery."

Jennie sighed. "What is Detective Griffin going to do with the new evidence?"

"What can he do? They are both dead."

"Will he tell the public?"

"No. He will document everything and seal the records."

"Sounds like a cover up."

"It won't be the first one," Peter said.

Jennie clasped her hands. "I suppose so. Anything else?"

"He asked if Brenner revealed anything to me about the murders."

"What did you tell him?"

Peter's eyes shifted away from hers. "Nothing. I knew absolutely nothing about them."

"Looks like no one knows for sure."

"Only Dr. Levin and Brenner. It appears the answers were buried with them."

Jennie let out a deep breath. "The nightmare is finally over."

"Hope so."

"You sound skeptical."

"I don't believe we have seen the last of Detective Griffin," said Peter. "He'll never stop looking for answers."

"As long as there is nothing to find, why worry about it?"

Peter patted her hand. "You are right. We don't need to be concerned any longer."

Chapter Thirty

Jennie made a phone call. "Peter, come on over. I have something to show you."

A few minutes later Peter was by her side. He drew some deep breaths. "Did something bad happen?"

Jennie grabbed his hand and led him to the den. Chad was sitting on Martha's lap smiling.

Peter looked around the room. "What is it? I don't see anything wrong."

Jennie took Chad and set him on all fours. He crept along the floor then fell on his side.

"Surprise," Jennie said. "He is learning how to crawl. Isn't it wonderful?" She turned him around and set him on all fours again. He crawled up to Peter.

"Hi, sport." Peter grinned. "You move like a running back." He picked Chad up and bounced him on his knee. "You are getting to be such a big boy."

Chad grinned and cooed to Peter.

"He is such a joy," Peter said. "You are lucky to have him, Jennie."

"I know. I count my blessings every day."

Martha headed for the kitchen. "Are you staying for dinner, Mr. Johnston?"

"I don't think so."

"Please, stay," said Jennie. "Chad wants you to."

"In that case, yes."

Martha put Chad in his high chair and fed him some baby food.

"What an appetite," Peter said. "He eats like a running back, too."

"Martha prepares all his food. Nothing comes out of a jar," said Jennie. "You know what a good cook she is."

"The best."

When they finished eating, Martha cleared the table and went into the kitchen.

Peter looked at Jennie. "I haven't seen you drink in a long time."

"Not since I got pregnant." Jennie gazed at Chad. "I wanted my baby too much to take risks."

"That's great," said Peter. "What about now. Do you ever get the urge to drink?"

"Never. I don't need it anymore." Jennie smiled. "I live for Chad now."

"Do you know why you had a drinking problem before?"

"Because I was frustrated and unhappy with Brenner most of the time."

"Why?"

"He had difficulty making love to me," Jennie said. "I surmised he was seeing another woman."

"That's not true," said Peter. "I know for sure that you were the only woman in his life."

"He had a strange way of showing it."

Peter pondered for a moment. "I guess he had other problems."

Chad's chin dropped to his chest. "I have to put the little one to bed."

Jennie picked up Chad and started toward the bedroom. "Come say goodnight to him, Peter."

He followed her into the room. "Isn't it about time Chad had his own room?"

"After all that has happened, I can't bear to have him far away from me."

"Are you going to have him next to you when he grows up?" asked Peter.

Jennie laughed. "He'll be in his own room when the time is right."

Shortly after Jennie lay Chad in his crib, he was fast asleep. Peter kissed his forehead and headed toward the door.

Jennie sat on the bed. "You forgot to kiss me."

Peter sat beside her and gave her a peck on the cheek. "Goodnight, princess. Pleasant dreams."

Jennie threw her arms around his neck and kissed him with passion. "I've got to have you, Peter."

"We can't do it here. What if Chad wakes up?"

"He won't. Nothing wakes him up."

"What about Martha?"

"She never comes in here at night. But if she did, she would be thrilled."

"Oh, sure."

"She adores you," Jennie said. "Now shut up and kiss me."

While their hot lips met, Jennie slipped off her clothes and unzipped Peter's pants. In minutes, their naked bodies met in unity.

"My darling, you feel wonderful," Jennie said.

"So do you," whispered Peter while he kissed Jennie tenderly from head to toe.

They made love until their bodies shuddered in pure ecstasy.

Jennie moaned. "Make love to me again, please."

After a second time, they lay still in each other's arms. Peter glanced at the crib. Chad was wide-eyed. "Look. Chad is awake. He must have seen us."

"He can't talk, remember? Besides, the only thing he witnessed was his mother and father making love."

"What do you mean, mother and father?"

"That's right. You are Chad's father."

"Don't make jokes, Jennie. Brenner was his father."

"No, darling, Brenner was sterile. He pretended to be the father to save his image."

"But how...when did it happen?"

"Remember that time I stopped by to see you at your place when Brenner was away?"

"One night?"

"That is all it takes. Look into Chad's eyes."

Peter gazed into them. "Hard to believe. It is like looking into a mirror."

"Do you need a blood test to prove he is yours?"

"That won't be necessary."

Peter embraced Jennie and stared at Chad. "That beautiful baby is mine, ours. What a thrill."

"Do we announce it to the whole world?" Jennie asked.

"I would love to. I want to shout it from the roof tops, but you know that is impossible."

"I understand. You are the president now and have to protect your image."

Peter kissed her cheek. "You and I know the truth. That is all that matters."

Jennie hugged him. "You are right."

"What about Brenner?" Peter asked. "Did he know I was the father?"

"No."

"When did he find out he was sterile?"

"He was told years ago, and he had it confirmed after he found out I was pregnant."

Deep lines penetrated Peter's forehead. "Didn't he ask who the father was?"

"Yes, but I refused to tell him," said Jennie. "To protect him from scandal, he alleged the baby was his. In turn, he promised to take care of me."

Peter sighed. "It was best that he didn't know."

Jennie scowled. "Tell me something. Why are you so concerned about Brenner and what he knew about Chad?"

"I did work with the guy. Can you imagine if he knew I slept with his wife?"

"I don't think he would have cared."

Peter stood up. "This has been quite a night. I've got to go back to my place and do some thinking."

"What is there to think about?"

"Chad and what is best for him."

"Do you have any ideas?"

He shook his head. "No more talking. I am overwhelmed."

Peter kissed Chad and Jennie and with a pounding heart and a swirling head, he sped out the door.

Jennie lay back on her bed and peeked at Chad. "Baby, I believe you are about to get a daddy. Then you will have to get your own room."

Chad smiled and closed his eyes.

Chapter Thirty-One

Peter stopped by every night, had dinner, and played with Chad. One evening Peter and Jennie made love and were lying quietly in each other's arms.

"A poll was taken regarding you and me," Peter said.

Jennie laughed. "What kind of poll?'

"To see if the American people want us to get married."

Jennie sat up and peered down at him. "And the results?"

"It was unanimous. They said we should get married."

Jennie folded her arms. "Mr. Johnston, is this a proposal?"

"Let us just say, we have to please the people."

"You want to marry me to please the people?"

"Not exactly. Chad needs a father."

"That's it?"

"Yes. What do you say?"

Jennie pointed her chin toward the ceiling. "No."

"What do you mean, no?"

"What about me? How do you feel about me?"

"You should know by now."

Jennie pouted. "No, I don't know. Tell me."

Peter knelt on the floor and took her hand. "My dearest, Jennie. I love you with all my heart and want to spend the rest of my life with you." He kissed her hand. "Will you marry me?"

Jennie smiled. "Since you put it that way, yes."

They embraced. "I love you, Peter," Jennie said.

He looked over at Chad who was sitting in his crib. "How about you, guy? You want mommy and daddy to get married?"

Chad bounced up and down, grinned, and said, "Da-da."

"His first words," said Jennie. "Did you hear what he said?"

"Did he say, da-da?"

"That's what I heard."

Peter slipped one hand through Chad's and the other through Jennie's. "Let's set that wedding date now."

Jennie winked at Chad.

Six months later, Jennie viewed herself in the mirror. A long white gown fit her tall, curved body perfectly. Her shimmering auburn hair swerved in soft curls to the top of her head.

"You look absolutely beautiful," Nikki said. "I am proud to be your maid of honor."

"Thank you. You look lovely yourself." Nikki and the other four attendants were dressed in full-length shrimp-colored gowns with headdresses of shrimp and white roses.

"It's time to go," said Nikki.

Jennie took a deep breath and exhaled. "I'm so nervous."

"That's natural. You'll be fine."

Jennie met her father and walked slowly down the aisle.

All heads turned while many of them gasped. "What a beautiful bride."

Jennie stood next to Peter. He whispered in her ear. "You are gorgeous, princess."

"And you're my handsome prince."

They gazed into each other's eyes and repeated their marriage vows. Flashes from cameras lit up the church as Peter and Jennie kissed. Secret service men surrounded them as they entered a limousine. People lined the streets with happy faces, anxious to get a peek at the famous newlyweds. They waved, cheered, and blew kisses when the handsome couple rode by.

The driver pulled up to a side entrance of the White House. Jennie and Peter were led into a large ballroom. The room was decorated with multi-colored streamers and balloons. In the middle of the room was a six-foot wedding cake. Red, white, and blue icing circled each layer and met the figurines of a bride and groom on top. Hundreds of people were seated. Relatives from both sides, the administration, senators, and congressmen were present.

Loud applause broke out when the president and first lady appeared and walked toward the head table. The couple smiled, waved, and sat down. Champagne was poured into each glass. The newlyweds stood up and led everyone in a toast. Jennie pretended to drink hers, set it down, and requested water instead.

"One drink shouldn't hurt," Peter said.

"I don't want to chance it," said Jennie. "I've done so well. I hate to mess up now."

Peter patted her hand. "Smart girl."

Waiters and waitresses delivered huge plates of food to the bridge and groom and the rest of the head table. They continued until everyone was served.

After the tables were cleared, the band started playing, "I Believe in Miracles." Jennie and Peter got up to dance. The song was almost over when Jennie felt a tugging of her gown. She stopped dancing, looked down, and saw Chad with his little arms up in the air. She picked him up and put him between herself and Peter. People laughed and clapped as they danced around the room. They danced a couple of more numbers with Chad then brought him back to Martha.

"What a beautiful family. I'm so happy for you," Martha said. She wiped tears from her cheeks.

"We're happy, too," grinned Jennie.

The remainder of the afternoon was spent dancing and mingling with guests.

Jennie had just finished dancing with her father when Peter grabbed her hand and led her back to the dance floor. He held her close while they danced to a love song.

Peter whispered in her ear. "Let's get out of here."

"How can we do that?"

"Watch me."

Peter stopped to talk to four secret service agents. "Meet us at the end of the ballroom."

'Yes, sir."

The couple danced to the end of the room, opened the doors, and slipped into the hallway, followed by the agents. Within twenty minutes the bride and groom were changed into casual clothes and headed for a limousine, with the secret servicemen leading the way with their suitcases.

Once inside the vehicle, Jennie leaned her head back on the thick cushioned seat. "What an exciting day. It was just perfect, don't you think?"

"Couldn't have been better."

"Mrs. Peter Johnston. I love it." She kissed his cheek and put her head on his shoulder.

Peter put his arm around her and kissed her long and hard. "My beautiful princess. I love you so."

They left Washington D.C. and entered Virginia. In a short while they pulled up to a dock where a huge yacht was anchored alongside it.

"Why couldn't we have gone on a commercial cruise ship?"

"How much privacy would we have had?" asked Peter.

"None, I guess."

"This will be fun," Peter said as he got out of the car.

"Yeah. You and I and four secret service agents. Wow."

"Would you rather go back to our place?"

"No. I was only kidding." She took Peter's hand and got out of the limousine.

"I'm looking forward to having no people around us, aren't you?"

"Of course," Jennie glanced at the agents near them. "Except for our watchdogs."

"You should be accustomed to them by now."

Jennie shook her head. "I will never get used to them."

They boarded the magnificent yacht. The captain gave them a tour of the boat. Each agent had his own room that included a bathroom. The kitchen was bright with red and white wallpaper decorating half the walls, and oak paneling the other half. An oak dining set was in the center of the kitchen with a stove and refrigerator along one of the walls. There was a deck, including cushioned furniture, in the front of the yacht to view the trip.

The captain showed Peter and Jennie their bedroom, the largest one, with their own private bathroom. In the middle of the floor was a hot tub.

"Peter, look. Our own zacuzzi."

"Fabulous."

"I'm glad we are going on this yacht," Jennie said. "It is going to be fun."

"Told you so."

In minutes they were headed out to sea.

"Where are we going again?" asked Jennie.

"The Caribbean."

"I have never been there. Will we stop anywhere?"

"Our destinations are Playa del Carmen, Cozumel, Grand Cayman and Montego Bay, depending on how many people recognize us."

"Maybe we can wear disguises."

"We may have to."

Jennie smiled. "Sounds thrilling."

"I'm sure you'll love it."

"I agree, but right now I'm starved," said Jennie. "Is there any food here?"

"I'll find out." Peter picked up the phone and called the captain. He turned to Jennie. "Do you want to eat in the kitchen or our room?"

"Here."

Peter put down the phone. "It will be ready in a half hour."

They enjoyed a seafood meal thirty minutes later.

"This is wonderful," Jennie said. "They say seafood makes you passionate. Think so?"

"I've never heard of that but, if so, I am looking forward to tonight."

Jennie tested the door to ensure it was locked and went into the bathroom.

Shortly afterwards she appeared and stood in front of Peter. She wore a transparent black teddy and long black stockings that were held up by a garter belt.

Peter gazed at her. "Wow!"

"Like it?" asked Jennie with a sultry voice. She edged slowly toward her husband.

"Love it." He opened up his arms. "Come to me, my sexy one." Jennie slithered into his arms. Peter picked her up and put her on the bed. He got undressed and carefully took off Jennie's teddy and garter belt, then pulled off the stockings that covered her shapely legs, while kissing every part of her body along the way.

"Baby, this is heaven," Peter said as he made love to his new wife.

"Yes. Oh, yes," she moaned.

They lost count of the times they made love, with each experience slower, and more sensuous.

Jennie sat up and ran her fingers along Peter's face. "You remind me of a rabbit the way you move. Did anyone ever call you Peter Rabbit?"

"No, but someone I loved and felt very close to at one time, had a special name for me."

"Really? What was it?"

Peter put his finger on her lips. "You have to promise never to tell anyone."

"I promise. Tell me, please."

He pulled her head down and whispered in her ear. "Bunny."

Jenny gasped. "Brenner was calling out to Bunny at the hospital. That was you." Her eyes bulged. "You and Brenner were lovers, weren't you?"

Peter shrugged his shoulders. "You knew all along."

"Oh, my God!" She gaped at him. "Tell me the truth. Is that why Brenner had all those people killed, to cover up your affair?"

Peter nodded, then glared at her. "Don't worry, my dear. No one will ever know, will they? And remember, the case is sealed."

His new bride cried out while his hand quickly muffled her scream.

About the Author

Because her mother always worked while she was growing up, Louise was alone for long periods of time, which stimulated a vivid imagination. She dreamed of being rich with the ability to travel to intriguing places all over the world.

Her fascination with books filled many hours. BAMBI, BLACK BEAUTY, and the YEARLING were among her favorites.

During the years that followed, she received a degree in education, married her childhood sweetheart, and had four beautiful children. Thirteen years later the marriage ended. After she raised her children, she remarried and moved to Florida.

During several years of substitute teaching, she had a burning desire to write. She enrolled in a few writing courses and pursued that goal. After completing her courses, Louise sold her first book-length manual, HOME-BASED ADVERTISING SERVICES. One of her short stories, "A Better Way," appeared in the magazine, Home Life.

Louise dared to dream, to fulfill her dream, doing what she loves best…writing.

www.ingramcontent.com/pod-product-compliance
Lightning Source LLC
Chambersburg PA
CBHW020435290526
45785CB00002B/865